IT'S NOT MY FAULT

THE  FOR
OVERCOMING LIFE'S OBSTACLES

DR. HENRY CLOUD
DR. JOHN TOWNSEND

THOMAS NELSON
Since 1798

NASHVILLE DALLAS MEXICO CITY RIO DE JANEIRO

Published in Nashville, Tennessee, by Thomas Nelson. Thomas Nelson is a registered trademark of Thomas Nelson, Inc.

Thomas Nelson, Inc., titles may be purchased in bulk for educational, business, fund-raising, or sales promotional use. For information, please e-mail SpecialMarkets@thomasnelson.com.

Published in association with Yates & Yates, LLP, Literary Agent, Orange, California.

Scripture quotations marked (NIV) are taken from The Holy Bible, New International Version®. © 1973, 1978, 1984 by International Bible Society. Used by permission of Zondervan. All rights reserved. Scripture quotations marked (NASB) taken from the New American Standard Bible®, © 1960, 1962, 1963, 1968, 1971, 1972, 1973, 1975, 1977, 1995 by The Lockman Foundation. Used by permission. Scripture quotations marked (NLT) are taken from the Holy Bible, New Living Translation. © 1996, 2004. Used by permission of Tyndale House Publishers, Inc., Wheaton, Illinois 60189. All rights reserved.

Cover Design: John Hamilton | JohnHamiltonDesign.com
Cover Image: Janusz Kaphsta / SIS
Cover Photo: Images.com
Interior Design: Inside Out Design & Typesetting

ISBN 978-0-7852-8939-5 (tradepaper)
ISBN 978-1-5914-5473-1 (hardcover)

Printed in the United States of America
10 11 12 13 14 QW 9 8 7 6 5 4 3 2 1

This book is dedicated to all those who cope
with other people's blame and those who want to
deal with their own. May you find solutions
for your struggles and accomplish your dreams.
God bless you.

Contents

Acknowledgments

The authors would like to thank the following people who helped make this book a reality:

Sealy Yates and Jeana Ledbetter, our literary agents: As always you provided guidance and direction throughout the process far above and beyond the call of duty. Thanks for your commitment to getting this book through the "hoops."

Byron Williamson and Joey Paul: Thanks to you both for getting the idea and wanting it to happen. Byron: Your vision and creativity helped drive and shape the initial conceptualization. Joey: Your care and competency kept the process on track for us.

Rob Birkhead: Thanks for all your artistical talent which provided a great graphical way to convey the ideas.

Tom Williams, Anita Palmer, and Jennifer Day: Your attention to meaning and clarity greatly improved the readability of the book.

The staff of Cloud-Townsend Resources: Maureen Price, Steffanie Brooks, Jodi Coker, Kevin Doherty, Belinda Falk, Erin Kershaw, Debra Nili, Kris Patton, Patti Schenkel, Edrey Torres and Melanie Whittaker. We appreciate your diligence, values, and humor.

John would like to acknowledge the following people:

My executive assistant Janet Williams: Your conscientiousness and concern have made my work doable for me.

My wife Barbi and our sons Ricky and Benny: Thanks again for being such an awesome, caring, and growing family.

Introduction

It has been said that there are two kinds of people in the world: those who get what they want, and those who don't. Winners and losers. Haves and have nots. And the sad thing is that some people feel that they are stuck in the wrong group and forever destined never to get what they want out of life.

In reality, however, it is not that black and white. While there are some clear winners and losers, more often we see that most people have some areas of life where they are able to make it all work, and other areas where they are stuck. Since you are reading this, it is doubtful that everything in your life is failing. It is likely, however, that there *is* some area where you have not quite been able to close the gap between what you desire and the results you are actually getting. If that is the case, this book is for you.

While it is not altogether true that people can be divided into two types clearly labeled winners and losers, they can be divided into two types in another way. And which of those types you are *will absolutely determine whether or not you find more of what you want in life.* What are the two types?

Those who take responsibility for their lives, and those who don't.

That is the topic of this book. We can assert with the utmost confidence, from both research and experience, that the information and guidance we'll give you in these pages has the power to transform not only those areas where you are stuck and want to get moving, but even seemingly hopeless situations. This is not just theory. This No-Excuse Plan has been proven to work for as long as history has kept records of changed lives.

Winners in a Culture of Blame

We live in a culture of blame. People will blame anyone or anything for their misery sooner than take the responsibility to own it and make it better. Blame has become institutionalized in our courts, legislatures, and schools; it pervades our psychology and medical thought and even our moral and spiritual lives. The result? More people with more misery, but always with someone or something else to blame it on.

While blame may ease some of the anxiety, guilt, fear, or sense of responsibility, *it does nothing to solve the problems.* As long as we think, feel, or act as if there is nothing we can do about whatever we struggle with, we will remain stuck.

You probably know or have known people who always have an

excuse, never taking ownership for what they could do to make their situation better. If you know such a person, then you know the frustration of trying to help someone who will not take responsibility. As psychologists, we have seen it a thousand times. Often, within the first five minutes of talking with someone, we can tell that solving his or her problem is going to be a long, uphill battle. Not because the particular problem itself is unsolvable or the condition untreatable, but because the most important factor required for overcoming it is missing: the ability to take responsibility for one's own life.

On the other hand, when someone *does* have that one ingredient—the ability to take responsibility—we have more than just a vague hope for him or her. *We know that this person will get better.* It borders on absolute certainty.

And that is what we believe about you as well. If you are willing to do what all the winners in the world do in that area of your life that seems stuck, then your future can be different. Taking responsibility in this way does not at all imply that your situation is your *fault* or that you caused it. It only means that since you find yourself in it, you are willing to put your arms around it and take ownership to make it better.

We understand that it sometimes takes more than just willingness. There are willing, responsible people who sometimes remain stuck. But in those cases, the missing ingredients are usually the information, guidance, and resources necessary to bring about change. And we will help you by supplying those very items. We will join your willingness to take ownership of your life, even if you did not cause your problem or situation, and we will guide you in taking the steps that can lead you to the place where you want to be. Sometimes all it takes for good, responsible people to take ownership of a situation and make a change is just to know what the next steps are.

For example, a person may be in a relationship with someone who truly is a "problem." It really *is* the other person's fault. But even when dealing with a problem person, you will learn that if you just know what responsible steps to take from your side, you can change a relationship and sometimes even turn the person around. Or if you know what responsible steps to take in a situation like depression or anxiety, where the symptoms are sometimes caused by trauma or bad treatment from others, you can change a situation that you did not cause.

FINDING THE MISSING PIECE

Whether it involves a clinical issue, such as depression, anxiety, or addiction; a relational problem, such as marriage or dating; or a career that will not get moving—if you are willing to be the kind of person who takes responsibility for what you *can* do and change your focus from what you *cannot* control, you can improve the situation or solve the problem. God designed you to be able to do that, and he will empower you to bring it about.

So, to both kinds of people reading this book—those who have not yet taken responsibility for their lives, and those who are ready to do it but do not know what to do in a particular situation—we invite you to read on. Discover how *responsibility* is not a negative word, but the one piece that has been missing in your quest to realize your dreams and desires.

Henry Cloud, Ph.D.

John Townsend, Ph.D.

1

You Can Own Your Own Life

1

Excuses change nothing, but make everyone feel better.
—MASON COOLEY

Where should the line be drawn between an individual's own responsibility to take care of herself and society's responsibility to ensure that others shield her?"

What do you think these words could be referring to? What evil does the questioner suggest is lurking out there that society needs to come to grips with so you and I will be safe?

Nuclear war? I agree. A society should place the responsibility on its own shoulders to protect us all from nuclear holocaust. How about serial killers? Another good guess. The FBI spends a lot of time and resources taking responsibility for making sure that you are safe from the Hannibal Lecters of the world. What about an outbreak of bird flu, E. coli, or some other deadly disease? Right again. The U.S. Centers for Disease Control has your back covered.

So which of these mortal dangers was the opening quote referring to when it asked where society should step in and make sure that you are okay?

The answer: *none*. Guess what the culprit was that spawned this quote. I will give you a hint. The quote comes from a ruling by a United States Federal judge. Still wondering?

The perpetrator so dangerous that protection from it may require the collective power of our entire society is—

a McDonald's hamburger.

Just think. It took a judge in United States Federal Court to figure out the answer to that question. Why? Because two girls were overweight and claimed that McDonald's was responsible for their eating habits. The attorney for the plaintiffs argued that McDonald's food was "physically or psychologically addictive." From that perspective, the poor girls just did not have a chance. The Golden Arches reached out and grabbed them, pulled them in, and force-fed them.

But, common sense—and as we shall argue—the created order, prevailed. Part of the judge's opinion held that "if consumers know (or reasonably should know) the potential ill health effects of eating at McDonald's, they cannot blame McDonald's if they, nonetheless, choose to satiate their appetite with a surfeit of supersized McDonald's products."[1]

Thank you, Judge, for bringing some sanity to this picture. But it begs a bigger question. How did we get to the place where someone would even think that they could sue a hamburger chain for their weight problem? Was it the permissive sixties that did away with personal responsibility in our culture? Was it humanism that said humanity is basically good and it is our poor environment that causes us to make mistakes? Was it permissive parenting that taught an entire generation to think that nothing is its responsibility—nothing bad that happens is ever my fault? Was it the psychologists who said that to discipline a child might hurt his self-esteem? Or was it all those hamburgers we ate that made us think this way?

Actually, as much as we like to talk about how far society has gone astray (and there is truth to that), blaming others is not a new problem created by twenty-first century America. Though we do seem to have perfected blame as a cultural and legal art form, it is not a modern phenomenon. In fact, it has been part of human nature from the beginning of time.

When God asked Adam the equivalent of "Why did you eat the hamburger?"—in Adam's case the forbidden fruit—Adam quickly blamed his wife: "The man said, 'The woman you put here with me—she gave me some fruit from the tree, and I ate it'" (Genesis 3:12 NIV).

When God asked Eve about the issue, she offloaded responsibility in a similar fashion. "Then the LORD God said to the woman, 'What is this you have done?' The woman said, 'The serpent deceived me, and I ate'" (Genesis 3:13 NIV).

All Adam needed was an attorney and he could have sued God, Eve, and the serpent. Or maybe they could have bonded together and filed the first class-action suit. But the truth is that there is a fundamental problem with human nature, as philosophers, psychologists, and theologians have noted for centuries. The problem is simply this: *we fail to take responsibility for our own lives.*

We shift the blame, and the responsibility, to others. It is just a part of who we are, and it has been that way from day one. We did not learn it from our environment, although our environment can augment it. Instead, we bring it into the world as a tendency that comes with being human.

Now, certainly we have *reasons* why we do not take ownership for our own behavior and lives. Adam and Eve did it, in part, because they were ashamed and afraid. Those are big reasons for us as well. No one ever said that we blame for no good reason. Even the girls in the McDonald's lawsuit had struggles and determinants that were making self-control difficult for them. There is no doubt about that. Perhaps they felt ashamed, powerless, or afraid. Anyone who thinks they are going to help an overweight person by just saying, "It is your choice. Stop eating," has either never been overweight or has never worked with many overweight people or addicts. External factors do influence our behavior. Even the Bible affirms that.

But, the fact that there are reasons that drive us to do things, and the question of whether we are responsible for what we do with that are two very different matters. The bottom line is this: No matter what reason drives someone to overeat, whether it's stress, McDonald's advertising, boredom, lack of education, a bad childhood, or whatever, there is still a reality: *if you overeat, you will gain weight.* The "why" you did it, no matter how valid, will not solve the problem. The same thing happens in people's lives every day. *When we succeed in blaming someone for our problems, we still are no closer to a solution for them.* Still, we do it anyway to make ourselves feel temporarily better. And when we do, we still have the problems.

If these girls had won their lawsuit, it would have been the worst thing that could have happened to them, for it would have reinforced the belief that someone else was in control of their behavior. Thus, it would have gotten them no closer to solving their weight problem.

It may have helped the girls feel better in some way to have been awarded a big settlement for McDonald's having made them fat. They might have temporarily gotten over some bad feelings about being overweight. I don't know them, so I can't say. But, I can say one thing: they would not have been one step closer to being a normal weight. Not one ounce. Not one fraction. Why? *Because they are the only ones who can do anything about the real problem. They are the only ones who can refuse to eat the burgers.* They are the only ones in control of that. And in the end, it is all about control. Who ultimately has it? As we shall see, that is ultimately the only thing that matters.

It Is All About Control

I know a man whose childhood was not the greatest. His mother used him for her own needs and his father did not provide the crucial support to give him confidence to accomplish his dreams. In very real ways, he was shortchanged. Now he works at a job that he doesn't like and dates a woman who treats him much like his parents did. She uses him and is not supportive.

Every time he thinks about his hated work or his poor relationship, he reacts in a familiar pattern. He gets bugged and complains. None of his problems are his own fault. He complains about how the company doesn't care about him, and how they use their employees for their own ends. And he complains about how his girlfriend thinks only about herself, and how she always gets her own way. When I asked him about looking for a new job, he said his girlfriend has a lot going on right now, and he spends so much time helping her that there's little left for job hunting. "Plus," he said, "they really aren't hiring in my field right now."

"What about another field?" I asked. "What about your interest in computer science that you told me about?"

"Well, I would have to get another degree," he said.

"Yeah, so why don't you do that?" I asked.

"Well, you know how schools are with mid-career people. They don't like to admit students into those adult programs without experience in the field. The ones with the experience are the ones who get the spots," he said.

Thus the conversation continues in an endless circle. Finally I give up. *Poor guy*, I think to myself. *He's stuck in a prison.* But the thing about his prison is that he is the one who holds the key, and yet he doesn't know it. He is the one in control of his life and yet he feels as if everyone else is. He is the only one who can do anything about his problems, and yet he is the one who says he can't do anything. From his perspective, his troubles are not his fault. If only his girlfriend would become less needy and demanding; or if only his company would care and do more for him; or if only colleges would get more understanding—only then would his life ever be different. It is always up to someone else to make it better. And since they don't, it gets no better.

Now, if you were to ask him, he would not say this outright. But that is, in effect, what he *is* saying and living out each day. For, if his girlfriend, his employer, and the college are the reasons that things are not better for him, then his only hope of anything ever getting any better is that they change for him. In his mind, they have all the power and control over his life.

The overweight girls had the same attitude. "If McDonald's made me this way, then my only hope is for McDonald's to do something to make me different." Guess what. Neither McDonald's, my friend's girlfriend, his company, or the colleges are holding meetings right now on how they plan to make these people's lives different. The people themselves are the only ones who can do that.

I have another friend from a similar background. Very little support, encouragement, or help from her family. They hurt her in two ways: first, by the various harmful things that they inflicted on her. And second, by depriving her of the good things she needed. But her reaction was quite different from that of the first friend I mentioned.

Somewhere along the line she learned the difference between what happens to us and what we do with it. She learned that it's not the bad things that happen to us that determines our destiny; it's how we respond to them. She learned that no one can have control over your life if you do not let them. In short, she learned that she "owns" her life, not someone else. And it is the owner who has the rights.

She learned that if her family did not provide the support and validation she needed, she was free to find it from other people. And she did. She joined a spiritual community that loved her and supported her. From that base, she grew to be emotionally strong. Although her parents inflicted lots of emotional pain on her, she learned that she was free to find help in dealing with that pain, to learn new patterns of relating, and to get well. So she diligently went to sustained therapy, joined support groups, and overcame the significant pain in her life. Today she is very healthy.

Although this woman's parents did not support her intellectual pursuits in any form, including financially, she learned that she could make her own choices and take responsibility for those interests herself. So she got jobs, paid for school, and eventually achieved a graduate degree and became a professional in a high-paying field.

This woman also learned that no matter how hurtful one's relationships may be in early life, in your adult life you can choose relationships with people who will not be hurtful. She chose to marry a good, honest, and responsible man.

Even though God did not instantly deliver this woman from suffering the very moment she prayed, either in childhood or beyond, she learned that she did not have to choose to believe that he is not there or does not care just because healing is not instantaneous. Instead, she chose to believe what he says about our living in a world where people have freedom and choices, and sometimes they use that freedom to hurt us. She understood that he is not to blame for that. As a result, she kept alive a faith that led her to many experiences of his intervention, healing, and deliverance. She did not become bitter toward God or, like the Israelites facing the difficulties of the desert, give up her faith and abandon God. Instead, she became one of those who followed him *through* the desert to the Promised Land.

And, in what I think is her greatest *achievement*, this woman learned that although your own parents might not give you what you need in life, you do not have to continue that pattern and pass it to another generation. Instead, she gave her children great parenting, and they grew up to be healthy, responsible people.

Her life did not belong to her circumstances, her parents, her lack of resources, or her lack of options. Her life belonged to her. It was a gift from God. And she was not going to allow what had happened to her be in charge of the rest of her life. Just because how she was treated was someone else's fault, which it was, she did not wait for someone else to make it better. She owned her life. Even if she didn't cause the problems, she was proactive about solving them. She was in charge of what went on from that point forward. That was the difference between my two friends. One was a perpetual victim, and the other was a victorious person.

WHAT IS A PERSON?

In the beginning, the Bible tells us, God created people "in his image" (Genesis 1:27). This means a lot of things, but one thing stands out as it relates to our present subject: the ability to choose what one wants to be. This ability to choose is what is referred to as "will." Literally, the term "will" means "desire." But for humans created in God's image, it means much more than that. The animals have desire, or appetite. But only humans have the ability not merely to desire things, but also the *creative* will to take responsibility for that desire and bring about the achievement of it. That creative ability resides in the nature of God, and he has passed it on to us. Your dog is pretty much going to live where you decide he will live. But you, being human rather than canine, have a creative choice. God has delegated two things to you:

The ability to create and respond to life

The reality consequences of those choices

Often you cannot choose what happens to you. You cannot determine which cards you are dealt. But you can always do something:

You can always create, seek, and find a range of options to determine how you will respond to what happens, and how you will play the cards in your hand.

Adam did not choose how many trees were given to him in the garden. But, he did choose which to eat from. The girls in the lawsuit did not choose for McDonald's to make and advertise food that could make them gain weight. But, they did choose how they would respond to that advertising. My first friend did not choose parents who taught him what non-supportive relationships were like. But he did choose to find a girlfriend who was like them. Furthermore, he chose to allow her non-support and self-centeredness to control his life. He also chose to stay in the state that his family left him in rather than make an attempt to grow out of it. It was easier to blame than to change. As a result, he was choosing his life, one sentence of blame at a time.

We do not always like the enormous freedom to choose that we actually possess. It frightens us. It makes us responsible. But it is a reality. That freedom to choose is the element that explains the difference between my two friends. Both were from difficult backgrounds and faced difficult obstacles. But the way each chose to respond to those circumstances was very different. And their different choices created very different outcomes.

Each of us faces difficult circumstances in life. God grants each of us talents, brains, and abilities with which to meet them. And then he gives us the choice as to how we will respond. He gives us enormous freedom and responsibility. Listen to how this delegation of responsibility is described from the beginning:

> Now the LORD God had formed out of the ground all the beasts of the field and all the birds of the air. He brought them to the man to see what he would name them; and whatever the man called each living creature, that was its name. (Genesis 2:19 NIV)

God did not name the animals for Adam. What he did do was give Adam the creative ability to come up with options and name them. Had my first friend been the one in the garden, he might have said, "That's just like God, isn't it? Tells me to name all these creatures but doesn't even provide me with a list of possible names. How am I supposed to do this? He's so non-supportive. Maybe I'll sue him for a non-supportive work environment, lack of training, and poor employee assistance."

That is very much like what the loser in the responsibility lottery said in the parable of the talents. Remember the story? The master gives three people different amounts of resources to invest. The first two make their investments and get nice returns. The master rewards them with more resources. But the third was like my first friend. He blamed the master for not giving him what he thought he needed to make it work, so he did nothing with what had been entrusted to him. Listen to his words:

> Then the man who had received the one talent came. "Master," he said, "I knew that you are a hard man, harvesting where you have not sown and gathering where you have not scattered seed. So I was afraid and went out and hid your talent in the ground. See, here is what belongs to you."
>
> His master replied, "You wicked, lazy servant! So you knew that I harvest where I have not sown and gather where I have not scattered seed? Well then, you should have put my money on deposit with the bankers, so that when I returned I would have received it back with interest.
>
> "Take the talent from him and give it to the one who has the ten talents. For everyone who has will be given more, and he will have an abundance. Whoever does not have, even what he has will be taken from him. And throw that worthless servant outside, into the darkness, where there will be weeping and gnashing of teeth." (Matthew 25:24–30 NIV)

Notice something. God did not say, "What are you talking about? I have not been mean to you! I have given you everything you needed to be successful with your talent!" Nor did he say, "Gosh, you are right. It is tough to only have one talent. Here, I will do your work for you." Neither what God had given this man nor what he had not given him was the issue. The issue was just one thing: what had he done with what *was* given him? How had he used it? How had he responded to the options that were available to him? Had he tried his best and failed, he would not have been graded on the failure. He was graded simply on whether or not he had acted responsibly with what had been dealt to him.

When the man made excuses, accusing God of harshness to the point of expecting too much of a person, God could have said, "No, I am not harsh. I do not ask for a return where I have not given anything. Didn't I start you out with a talent?" But he didn't say this because *the issue was deeper than whether or not the servant had a good excuse.* In fact, God's answer to the man recognized that his excuses may have been real! But they didn't matter. He said that even if those things were true, the man still should have at least done *something*! At the very least he should have taken responsibility and put the money to some kind of use. In other words, *there is no excuse.*

Perhaps our excuses may somewhat define and describe our options, but they do not do away with our responsibility. We still have the freedom to respond to whatever comes our way, whether we get tons of talents or only one.

All of us have certain areas of our life in which we only get "one talent." And those are the areas where we will be most afraid to make a positive choice. But God has designed the universe in such a way that he expects us to use the freedom he has given us to take responsibility for our situation, find the possible options, and respond to them.

And the results of our choices will simply be what they are. He does not always shield us from bad results, although at times he may. Most of the time, he allows us to reap the rewards of our choices, whether positive or negative. He will not smile indulgently at our foolish choices and think he is responsible for bailing us out. In fact, that was part of the devil's temptation of Jesus. Satan told Jesus to just jump off the high precipice, and not to worry, because God would save him. He even used a Bible quote to back up his temptation. But Jesus came back with a very firm reinforcement of the principle of responsibility. "It says: 'Do not put the Lord your God to the test'" (Luke 4:12 NIV). It is not an act of faith to fail to take responsibility for our lives and then think that God is somehow responsible for the outcome.

It began with God giving Adam and Eve a Paradise along with the abilities to rule it, and then holding them responsible for what happened. That was simply the created order of things. And that created order still remains, although now it's marred and mixed up by sin. God gives us a life and various degrees of resources to manage it and cope with it. Sometimes he allows bad things to happen and offers us help and other ways out of, or through, the difficulty. But even when he helps us and gives us resources, he still requires responsibility from us to live our lives by making responsible choices, and the results will always testify to how well we make those choices.

This is not just some brand of theoretical theology. If you don't believe me, step on the scales and look at reality. McDonald's or not, the scales don't lie; our lives weigh-in at what they truly are. Reality is what it is. And much of what ultimately constructs that reality is our choice. Much of it is up to us.

How We Give Away Ownership by
Demanding that Life Be Fair and Just

When we think of the terms *just* or *fair*, we are thinking about the way life *ought* to be. The dictionary defines *just* as what is *right* or *deserved*. When you say, "He got his just desserts," you are saying he got what he deserved in the situation. He got justice, and justice is one of the most important concepts in the universe. One of the hallmarks of a spiritual person, according to the Bible, is practicing justice and seeking it for those who are not getting it, especially those unable to seek it for themselves.

But the very reason that God asks us to seek and practice justice is that we live in a world that does not operate justly. The stark reality is that the world as we find it today is not a just or fair place. It does not operate according to the rules of how things "ought to be." People often do not get what they deserve. In fact, people often get things they don't deserve, awful things that hurt them in significant ways. That is the reality we encounter in this world. And part of believing in God and serving him is to right anything we find that is hurting someone, thus dealing with this harsh reality.

People who own their lives own them in reality, not in the fantasy world of the way life *ought* to be. That means they take ownership of their lives in the world that is, not the world as they wish it were. They own the fact that we live in a world that is neither fair nor just, and they deal with that reality. They do not spend a lot of energy protesting that unfair reality, demanding that the world be different. They deal with their world as they find it. As a result, they are effective in finding solutions to life, even when life has dealt them hard realities that just "should not be."

Other people, however, do not face reality so realistically. They refuse to own their lives in this world in which they find themselves. They want a different world—one that is fair and just, where people do what they are supposed to do. They want a world where people treat them the way they are supposed to be treated, and where good things happen to good people and bad things happen to bad people. That is fair, and that is the way it should be.

That is a wonderful wish. That kind of world was God's desire for us from the beginning. But that is not the world as it is. God came to grips with the fact that sin had messed up the created order, and he offered forgiveness to imperfect people, along with a chance for them to work through the unfairness and injustice to achieve a fulfilling life. But some people never get it; they never come to grips with the fact that the world is no longer perfect. They still want it to be perfect and sit around protesting the fact that it is not. They blame others, sometimes even rightly so, for their situations. It's not their fault. And while they waste time thinking about how life *ought* to be, they remain stuck with their problems because they will not deal with reality as it really is.

Effective people are like my second friend. They desire justice and seek it. But when it does not show up, they do not remain stuck. They get active and find the best solution to their situation. They find answers that are not provided by those who are diminishing their lives with unfair burdens. Like God, they look at an imperfect world and deal with it. They don't get stuck in the "life ought to be fair, and I am going to sit here and demand that it is" syndrome. They choose the "when life is not fair, I will do everything in my power to find an answer to the problem at hand" attitude.

One day on our radio show, a woman called in and said that her mother had treated her miserably during the Thanksgiving holiday.

The caller had gone back to school and was pursuing her dreams, and her mother had criticized her for wasting time trying to improve herself. "My mom was so critical," she said. "She just said the meanest things, like, 'Why are you doing that? You'll never make a living in that field. You are too old for this. Why don't you just get a real job and get on with it?' It was horrible. She ruined my whole holiday."

Sensing that this caller was not a child, I said, "That's terrible. By the way, how old are you?"

"Forty."

"So, is this the same mother you have had all those forty years?"

"Of course."

"And is this the first time that she has ever been non-supportive or critical?"

"Why, *no*! She does this all the time. She is so mean. She always ruins my plans and dreams. She has never supported me."

"Hmm. And what was it about this particular holiday that made you think that she was going to magically change and be a different person?" I asked, adding gently, "Why did you expect that to happen? Who do you think the crazy one is here?"

The caller did not like my point, but she got it. Sure, her mother should be a supportive person. In a perfect world, everyone should have a supportive mother. But her mother wasn't, and everyone doesn't. So the caller was ruining her life by dealing with it in a "life should be as it ought to be" manner. Instead of telling herself, "My mother is not a supportive person, so I had better come to grips with that and take responsibility for my needs to be supported," she had plunged blindly ahead and acted in accord with the way that she wished the world was. As a result, she was disappointed.

If she had not held on to that fairness requirement, she could get on with life. Her call to me would have been different. I would have heard something like this:

"I just had the greatest holiday. After enrolling in school I went to see my mother. As usual, she ridiculed my decision and gave me a hard time over it. In the old days, I always wished for her to be supportive, and when she was not, I was always hurt and deflated. But now, instead of thinking that she should be something she is not, I got my support from friends who were able to give it before I visited my mother. So I didn't need to look to her for it. Instead, I was able just to be with her and love her as she is. I accepted her for who she is with her limitations and enjoyed her and the visit. As a result, I did not give her the power over my life that she used to have. It was a great holiday."

That, by the way, is an actual conversation I had with a real person who was the kind who takes ownership of her life. As a result, she is able to live and love in the way that God does, accepting people for who they are and reality for what it is. That's the only way to deal with life effectively.

The big lesson here is this: *deal with life as it is.* Do not get stuck in protesting reality for what it "ought to be." If you give up the demand that life and the people in it be something other than what they are, you will find creative solutions to every difficult situation. And you will be a more loving person.

And, before you get pessimistic that the person you care about can never change, that is not what we are saying. We'll have more to say later about how you can be an influence for change with people you love. But first, you must take ownership for your own situation, whatever it is. If your difficulty is a non-supportive husband or wife, accept the reality of the problem and take ownership of dealing with it. Then and only then will you be able to find the best solution. If you just remain stuck and complain that he or she ought to be different, and you remain powerless and miserable until that person changes, then you are stuck in a prison. Take back the power. You can be free from whatever situation surrounds you to the degree that you are willing to take responsibility and ownership for it, even if it's not your fault.

People turn bad relationships around every day. People turn bad backgrounds around every day. People turn their unfair lives around everyday. How do they do it? *By putting their arms around reality as it is, owning their situation, and taking responsibility for it.* Do that and you'll be way ahead of the world. And that is what this book is about—we want to awaken your power to thrive, in spite of less-than-ideal situations—whether they are bad relationships, bad backgrounds, or bad circumstances. It's all up to *you.* Only you can take the first step: you can choose to give up your demand that life be something that it is not and own it for what it is. Accept that reality, and stop protesting it. So, it's raining. You can get an umbrella and make a nice day out of it, or you can go out and complain about getting wet. It is up to you. Give up "fair" and get a life.

Owning that This Is Not the First Time

"Is this the first time that your mother has not been supportive?" I asked the caller.

"Is this the first time that you have dated someone who has not been able to connect?" I asked the single who was six months into a disappointing relationship.

"Is this the first time that you have fallen prey to a promise about a great new deal that didn't pan out?" I asked the businessperson who felt duped again.

"Is this the first time that your willpower and commitment have not gotten you the weight loss you expected?" I asked the woman who was discouraged about her failure at dieting.

I could go on, but you get the picture. It's the story of all of us. We have patterns of failure, and they work well. We do not need any new ones, for the old ones work just fine. Think about it. Look back at the failures you've experienced in relationships, moods, goals, careers, habits, or whatever. They all tend to follow the same path. Meet the guy, get enamored, have him chase you, adapt to whatever he wants, have a good season, he loses interest, you try to win him back, and then finally he is gone. And then repeat that in the next seven relationships.

Or, experience a strong desire for a certain relationship, have it disappointed, have the argument, get stuck in the conflict, become estranged, come back together and not resolve it, and wait for the next go-round.

There are many examples of these repetitive cycles, but the truth is what it is: we have patterns of failure. They are very predictable. Often when a couple comes to me for counseling, one of them will make an accusatory statement about the other. "Okay, stop," I will say. "Do you know what your partner is going to say or do in reaction to what you just said? Do you know already where this conversation is going?" Invariably the answer is *yes*. So, that brings up the obvious question: "Then why do you do it?"

And here is the answer: we slip into patterns of behaving and reacting that remain fixed until we observe them and change them. We put ourselves on autopilot. We abandon conscious control and just repeat the same things over and over again. That is our innate nature, and it won't change until we work on changing it. You've heard it said, the fool repeats his folly, or more graphically, the dog returns to its vomit. (See Proverbs 26:11.) This means that to the degree that we are not seeing our own patterns of behavior and taking responsibility for them, we are going to repeat them.

Ownership is seeing those patterns and taking responsibility for them. If you are continually disappointed by certain repeated situations, then it is time to recognize the unproductive pattern and take ownership. The old adage has some truth to it: "Once, shame on you. Twice, shame on me." In other words, anyone can get duped. But once we've been duped, we have to take ownership and responsibility for our reactions and expectations to prevent it from happening again.

Sometimes that means not placing ourselves in the same situation again, or at least, not with the same expectations. Think of the caller we met, the daughter with the demeaning mother. Either she could choose not to go visit her mother and not place herself in the same situation, or she could visit her but change her expectation that her mother would be supportive.

At other times, taking ownership means that we understand who we are dealing with. We understand them as they are, not as we wish them to be. We take ownership of the reality before we go about trying to improve it.

Maria had a husband who did not "get it." They had been married for five years, and she was constantly hurt and disappointed by his behavior. But when she reacted with criticism, he would invariably react right back, and they would find themselves in a quagmire which always sank her into hopeless despair.

But then she learned about patterns. She could see her pattern of repeatedly expecting him to be different than he was and then suffering again when he wasn't. Her first reaction was to pull back and think, "He is never going to be any different. It's hopeless." Given the amount of pain she had endured, I understood. She would have been justified in giving up. But she was strong enough not to give up and wise enough to look at her pattern for an answer. When she examined the pattern, she realized that the problem with it was not in wanting the situation to be better; it was in the futility of thinking that it would get better each time she and her husband had a confrontation. So she regrouped.

Since Maria's husband was open to change, although slow at bringing it about, she decided to stop the old pattern and try something different. She would establish a new pattern and simply accept the inevitable fact that he would be slow to get it and unenthusiastic in his response. She would wish and ask for more, but when he blew it she would understand and take in stride the fact that this was going to be part of the picture. Part of the new pattern would be dealing with that reality. She owned her situation and did not let it do her in or destroy her marriage.

Instead, she gave up her old pattern of reacting to his failures and got in control. From then on, when he became hurtful again she told him that she was going to go hang out with her support group and give him some time to think about his behavior. When he was ready to see it as a problem, she would be glad to talk to him.

Maria's new pattern allowed her to remain in control of herself instead of allowing his failures to have the power over her that they had had before. As a result, he was left to deal with his failures. By changing her pattern, Maria did two things: First, she kept herself from being as hurt by his failures by opening herself to the reality that existed instead of the reality of her wishes. She saw him as he was. Second, she took a stance that did not allow his problem to become her problem. By getting above his issue, she became an agent of positive change in their relationship.

Ask yourself this: *In the significant areas of life that I care about, what unhelpful patterns am I repeating?* When you discover such a pattern, you find an area of responsibility. You are not responsible for the bad things that happen to you, but you are responsible for the patterns you create in response to them. Find a pattern and you find an opportunity for growth, change, and power. If every time I drive by the Golden Arches I turn in and eat five cheeseburgers, I may do well to see a pattern and not drive that route. Understand your patterns and own them. When you do that, you will begin to see alternative choices. If every time you find yourself in situation *A* you do *B* and get negative results, you may do well to recognize that this is not just something that is happening to you. You may have some responsibility in it. And the good news is this: wherever you have responsibility, you have the opportunity for change, choice, power, and a new outcome. If—and that is a big *if*—you take responsibility for that pattern.

Recently I rejoiced at a friend's victory. He called another friend and said, "I want you to hold me accountable for my dating life. I see a pattern, and it is not getting me where I want to be. I keep going for women who don't have the values and character that I want long-term. I get too involved with them, they want me to commit, and I can't. So I break up and we both get hurt. I want to stop doing that. I want to get in a relationship with a woman who shares my values."

When I heard that, I had hope for my friend for the first time in four years. Finally, he sees the pattern. My guess is that by this time next year, he will be in a relationship with a woman who shares his values.

So find your pattern. We all have them in the areas where we are stuck. The person whose willpower repeatedly fails to keep her from succumbing to the Golden Arches is no different than the one who keeps getting hurt by a critical mother she continually thinks will be different, or the person who thinks the next impulsive scheme is going to work when the ten before did not. See the pattern and you will discover the place to change your life.

The Real Diversion

Why do we blame others or circumstances for what happens to us? There are lots of reasons. We will go into more of them later but one that we want to consider here is diversion. Diversion gets our attention off the fact that we have responsibility. It diverts us from having to do whatever we could to make the situation better. Making the situation better may involve a lot of work, pain, or change on our part. That is a big reason why more people do not do it. It's easier to divert attention from their responsibility by blaming. It is far easier to say, "The economy is bad, and there are no jobs," than to get a degree in another field or to knock on a few hundred business doors. It is far easier to say that one is unhappy because his or her significant other is not very relational than to learn new patterns of relating that could repair the relationship. It is far easier to give in to one more hamburger ad than to attend a few Weight Watchers meetings. Blame is a sort of comfort food for the soul. It diverts us from the effort of owning responsibility.

The problem is that like any other "comfort food," diversion by blaming does not do much for you in the end. Eat a few gallons of ice cream and you are no healthier than when you began. Indulge in a few gallons of blame and you are no closer to a solution than when you began. Blame is the worst of diversions. Not only does blame divert us from our responsibility, it diverts us from the real issue at hand: *what we are losing by not taking ownership of the problem.* In the end, solving the problem is what matters.

So change your focus. Instead of focusing on what is causing your misery, try something new: focus on your misery. Focus on the result of what you are doing. Focus on what your pattern and your blame are costing you. If you do that, the blame begins to fade into the background, as it has no meaning. If you look at the result, then the "why" is not important. What is important is the "what." Why the problem is there ultimately means nothing. Solving the problem means everything. So McDonald's or some other fast food is the *why* you are eating. The *what* is that you are overweight, and solving that problem is the only thing that matters. Blame only diverts us from the real issue, and that is the result we are getting from our pattern of behavior. When we see that, we will be motivated to change the result by doing something different.

Only you can do that. Only you can look at your life and ask yourself if you like the results you are getting. Only you can look at the fruit of your pattern of behavior, take ownership of it, and do something about it. If you keep dating the sort of people whose values disappoint you, only you can own responsibility for your choices and stop blaming the external world for the outcome. If you are not losing the weight you want to lose, only you can take ownership of your weight and choose to change your eating patterns. If you are not getting what you desire out of your relationships, only you can look at that result and do something about it.

EXCUSES DON'T CHANGE THINGS

Once when I was doing a dating workshop a woman said, "Well, it's difficult to find dates when you work as much as I do. I'm a career woman, and I am so busy that I just can't find time to meet new people."

My reply was, "So I guess only unemployed women find dates." She balked, but I went on. I told her that while her excuse may have made her feel better, it was not going to change her result. Then I listed about ten things that busy women do to meet new people and find good results. They join services, change their schedules, network better, go to new places, engage in personal growth to find out why they are not attracting the men that are around them, and so on. I had written a book on dating and knew the research exploring how men and women change their dating lives. It happens successfully every day. This woman did not like hearing this list; it destroyed her ability to hide behind her excuses.

There's one thing that people do not realize about excuses. They are usually true. But my response to that is, *So what?* Yes, your excuse is real. Now, given that, what are you going to do about it? Your excuses do not change one single thing. It is up to you to do that. Get past the excuses and get on with it.

- It is true that you do not have time to work out. *So what? What are you going to do about that?*

- It is true that you do not have a supportive church for your emotional issues. *So what? What are you going to do about that?*

- It is true that a particular person in your life is not giving you what you deserve. *So what? What are you doing to do to deal with that?*

- It is true that not one good, single eligible person is showing up at your door. *So what? What are you going to do about that?*

- It is true that your particular metabolism allows easy weight gain. *So what? What are you going to do about that?*

Remember, in the parable of the talents the one with no result had a good excuse. He did not have a lot to begin with, and according to him, his master was a tough sell. But God comes along and says, "So what? You should have faced that reality and done something with it."

The good news is this: *you can.* You can do something with your reality. Taking ownership and responsibility for your life does not mean that you have to fix it alone. God will be with you and will work miracles. He is a God who answers. He is a God who parts the Red Sea and feeds thousands out of a few fishes and loaves. But he also asks us to own our responsibility—to name the animals, to dig our talent out of the ground, and to make difficult relationships work. He invites us to do that. And if we do, he will do the things that we are unable to do. But he won't do the things that we can do for ourselves. That is the created order. God will do the "God things," and we have to do the "people things."

And here is even more good news: there is help even when we can't do the people things. Even if we can't say no to a hamburger with our name on it, God will help us develop that ability when we own that problem and begin to deal with it. He does not think we are going to be able to do things we can't do. Addicts who admit their powerlessness as the first step know this well. But when we can't do it, God does ask us to take responsibility and ownership of the situation and to ask for his help and the help of others.

If you take that first step, things can change. Or you can blame the hamburger. It is up to you.

2

You Can Learn to Think Differently

2

Brain: An apparatus with which we think we think.
—AMBROSE BIERCE

Ever since our boys were small, my wife and I (John) have tried to help them learn about being financially responsible and aware. The world is not very kind to young adults who don't understand money. I sometimes engaged the concepts in a joking way. For example, when I would get ready to leave the house on a Saturday to work at the office, one of them would say, "Why are you going to the office?"

"Because I need to finish a project."

"What if you didn't finish?"

"I wouldn't get paid for the work."

"What if that happened?"

"We wouldn't have money."

"What would happen then?"

"We wouldn't be able to pay for what we need."

"Then what would happen?"

"Then we couldn't live in our house."

"Where would we live?"

"In a tent."

"Oh."

We had this strange dialogue many times when the kids were young. And at the end, they would look at me quizzically, see that I was joking, and say goodbye as I took off for the office.

However, the older they got, the less they bought into my argument and the more they cut to the chase. Now, in their teenage years, it goes more like this:

"Why are you going to the office?"

"I need to finish a project."

"Don't even say tent, Dad. It's Saturday. You promised to take me to Best Buy. Let's go."

And the sometimes-workaholic father goes to Best Buy instead of to the office.

THINKING AND THE TRUTH

The tent story illustrates a type of distorted thought process called *catastrophic thinking.* People who practice catastrophic thinking look at a small problem and picture it escalating until they're sure it will result in a disastrous outcome. A missed payment will bring bankruptcy; a marital fight will end up in divorce; forgetting to take a pill will cause a hospitalization. Catastrophic thinking can cause serious problems in your ability to make empowering, ownership-type choices. It can paralyze you and keep you stuck in anxiety.

But catastrophic thinking is just one example of a bigger issue. Whether or not you go the tent route, you almost certainly have some sort of thinking problem, technically called *cognitive distortion*, which can hamper your pathway to success. In this chapter we will show you several types of cognitive distortion.

A great deal of helpful research has been done with cognitive distortions. Most cognitive experts agree that our brains sometimes automatically reach conclusions about things based on some habit or perception, rather than accurately relating to what is really going on. Though it seems to us that we are thinking factual reality, the truth is much more complex. Our thinking is colored by our primary relationships, experiences, our past, our development, the amount of stress we are under, and many other factors.

For example, suppose you are a woman having dinner with a man you are dating. During the evening, his wallet opens accidentally, spilling out a photo of a very attractive woman. When you see the picture you might think, *He has a relationship already, and he hasn't said anything about it. I am history with this guy.* But seconds later he picks up the photo and says, "This is my sister, I'd like you to meet her sometime." Relieved, you congratulate yourself for not speaking every single thought that passes through your mind.

When we take distorted thinking to the next level, to the level of important life goals, we begin to see how much it can affect whether you get what you want out of life. The very way people think can render them powerless and helpless, and lead them to blame others.

For example, sometimes people see themselves and their abilities in such a way that they feel they could never succeed. Others look at their options as severely limited. And others listen to their minds telling them that if they take a small risk, their world will fall apart. You really can't overstate the importance of your thinking patterns. Nor can you overstate how dramatically helpful it can be to learn to think differently. That is why thinking is one of your eight keys to empowerment and life change.

Make the Shift

As you begin the process of learning to think differently, one fundamental reality that you must come to terms with is that *your mind is not always telling you the truth!* Your thinker sometimes thinks thoughts that have nothing to do with reality. This is despite the fact that your mind may be telling you that those thoughts are real, true, and accurate.

This is not easy for most of us to accept. And it's no wonder, because all we have to think with is our mind, and most of the time, our mind operates as if its perceptions were true. Your mind doesn't usually say, *Look, it seems like your boss isn't seeing you in a positive light, and you need to do something about this. Maybe you should talk to him. But I could be all wrong. Maybe he really likes you. Maybe I'm a little bit paranoid, or maybe I don't want you to get set up and get too hopeful here. You know, you can't always trust what I, your mind, says. Anyway, good luck, and make your best choice.*

No, if your mind worked like this, you would have a hard time making any choices at all! Your brain thinks what it thinks, and it is usually fairly sure about its perceptions.

The bad news is that while your thinker always tends to come across as sure, it may not always be accurate. The good news is that you can change that. You can help your thinker to think in more reality-based, perceptive, and helpful ways about you and your life. In fact, *you, and only you can begin to think differently* in ways that are best for you. Rather than letting your thinking contribute to your difficulties, you can learn to use your thinking to your advantage and toward achieving your goals. This is an important issue, because so many of our decisions are based on what our thinker, the brain, tells us.

This doesn't mean that we can simply tell ourselves to think differently and it will automatically happen. You can't simply repeat the truth over and over and over and hope your thoughts get the message and make the change. That's not how it works. But you can make significant shifts, as we will show in this chapter, in how you look at life and yourself. And these shifts can result in changed thoughts.

Begin by making the essential first shift. Here it is: *give up the idea that what you think is always the way things are.* Question what your mind is perceiving, and learn the tips we will give you here to help train it to see what truly is.

This step is also good for your mental health. One of the primary indicators of a character problem is a person's resistance to questioning his perceptions about his situation or relationships. He is absolutely sure that things are the way he sees them.

Have you ever been in a relationship with a person who persisted in seeing you as the bad guy, no matter what evidence you gave to the contrary? New or different information had no effect—whether it proved that you weren't what he thought you were or that you had really changed. He was, as the saying goes, "always certain and often wrong."

A person with this sort of rigidity will inevitably have trouble reaching his goals. Reality is larger than we are, and when we insist that reality conform to our perceptions, we have the same mindset as the two-year-old who sees her parents as hateful because they won't give her a piece of candy. People who are into success bend their knees, and their perceptions, to reality. That is the mark of an adult, and not a child.

Further, the "always certain and often wrong" person will encounter great resistance, not only from reality, but also from healthy people who don't put up with foolishness. That person will end up losing business deals, having relational shipwrecks, and suffering for his or her rigidity.

I once consulted with a company whose CEO was "always certain and often wrong." He was a pleasant person, but he continually resisted the opinions and viewpoints of others in his group. In his mind, his perceptions were reality; there was no distinction between the two. For example, when two of his vice presidents confronted this CEO, showing how his approach to solving a marketing problem would not work, he said simply, "No, I'm sure it will work." Even in the face of spreadsheets and numbers, he could not imagine his viewpoint to be in error, though it was. As a result, the talented people in his group ended up leaving, feeling frustrated and not allowed to achieve their potential. The company suffered because the CEO couldn't imagine that his mind did not perceive absolute reality at all times.

Stay with us and we will help you make sure you're not in that camp.

What Your Mind Distorts

Let's look at some of the major ways that our mind distorts reality in the areas that affect empowerment and life ownership. As you read over these common statements or practices, think about times you may have used them yourself, and consider what it may have cost you.

Distorted-Thinking Statement No. 1: "I've Tried Everything and Nothing Helps."

When facing an unreached goal, a relational opportunity, or a life problem that needs to be resolved, a person will often express some form of *I've tried everything and nothing helps.* That is to say, he *believes* he has tried everything, and there are no solutions. In his mind, he has exhausted all the possibilities for making changes, achieving dreams, and making improvements, and now he must resign himself to the reality that there is no hope for betterment. Nothing helps.

It is true that there are those times in which nothing does help, at least in the sense that you can't undo the past. When a person you love dies, he is gone. When you get fired, you are not likely to get the job back. When your husband says critical things to you, they can't be unsaid. No device has yet been invented that can rewind what has happened and replay it by a different script. Dealing with the inevitability of the past is more a matter of knowing how to grieve and adapt.

But the distorted thinking that leads one to think everything possible has been done and the situation is hopeless is another matter. The person with this mentality believes he has nothing left but to accept a bad situation with no hope of change. That is a discouraging and disempowering thinking pattern, and it keeps people stuck and hopeless.

I can't count how many times a caller on our radio show has said, "I've tried everything to solve this problem, and nothing helps." She may be referring to a troubled marriage, a problem child, or a weight issue. The problems vary widely, but this distorted-thinking response to them is all too common. When I hear this distortion, I generally respond with two questions.

What is "everything"? More often than not, the caller will rattle off a pretty short list that doesn't even begin to exhaust the possible approaches to a solution. Say you have a husband with an anger problem. What have you done? Let's list some of the options. You could:

- Talk to him.

- Let him know specifically how his anger affects you.

- Ask him what he thinks is the problem.

- Invite him to tell you what he thinks might be your contribution.

- Change what you need to change, in his terms, not yours.

- Clarify your own distortions about appropriate and inappropriate anger.

- Tell him what specifics you want changed.

- Tell him not just what you don't want, but what you want.

- Work on increasing trust and attachment between yourselves as a couple.

- Pray together as a couple about the matter.

- Look at Bible passages that teach about anger.

- Help him learn about grief and sadness as an antidote to rage.

- Bring others into the picture to help.

- Go to a support group.

- Go to counseling.

- Warn of the consequences.

- Set limits.

- Set stricter limits when he escalates.

- Give affirmation when he is more self-controlled.

The list could go on. The point is this: if you find yourself saying you have tried everything possible, it's a good thing to question whether you really have.

The second question I ask when a caller tells me she has tried everything is, "What do you mean by 'try'?" I attempt to find out what the caller really means by her use of that word. For example, how many times did you tell your husband you wanted him to stop drinking? How direct, forceful, and serious were you with him?

Often I find that *try* means, "I brought it up once or twice, and I'm not really good at confrontation anyway, and he ignored me, so I decided that it wasn't working." But that interpretation of *try* doesn't take into consideration how much work it takes for people to change their behavior. It takes a lot of time and energy, and it often takes many repetitions and efforts to bring into his awareness that you intend to stay on the issue; it isn't going away.

Often, there is another factor driving the "I've tried everything" thinking. Sometimes an individual is afraid of failure, discouraged, or just plain worn out. Or he may feel that he is a pretty powerless individual in general and thus incapable of being an agent for change. If this describes you, it is worthwhile to dig out whatever is triggering this thinking and confront it in yourself.

Distorted-Thinking Statement No. 2: "I Can't"

I can't thinking is the opposite of *can do* thinking. It is literally *can't do* thinking. In this mentality, people feel unable to make any move to better their situation or reach their goal. They feel profoundly helpless. *I can't* thinking simply shuts the door to opportunities, hope, and change. There is no recourse; nothing can be done and nothing can be different.

Now, certainly there are some *can'ts* in the world. Most of us can't become NBA players, or Harvard professors, or Jack Welches. But the number of people endowed to achieve these goals is a tiny percentage of a tiny percentage of the population. There are a lot more *cans* than *can'ts* out there, but somehow for some people the *can'ts* seem to carry the day.

Here are some of the *I can'ts* that take over their thinking:

- Lose the weight.

- Get a better career going.

- Get my husband to listen to me.

- Confront my boss on this problem.

- Find the right person to date.

- Go back to school and retrain myself.

- Get my kids to mind.

If you have had these or similar thoughts, you are not alone. We all do from time to time. But when those thoughts become a pattern, it's time to see it as a problem.

Actually, there is a certain relief in *I can't* thinking. When people give up on a dream or on changing a problem situation, they feel they can stop beating their head against a tree. No longer must they keep making attempt after attempt. They give up, change directions, and change their focus and expectations.

This is well and good if you weigh 130 pounds and wanted to play in the NFL. It is probably wise that you changed your direction. But all too often the goal you walk away from may have been achievable, which means the relief of *I can't* is offset by settling for much less than you need to.

For example, a businessman friend of mine got involved in church a few years ago. He really loved God and wanted to grow in his faith. However, he had not grown up in the church. You may be aware of this, but sometimes churches unfortunately have their own "religious" language, with certain phrases and words, which has the result of keeping people feeling alienated rather than included.

My friend wanted to help out and serve, but he felt like he was at the bottom of the class because he didn't know "church language." He told me, "I like coming to church and learning, but I can't really help out. I don't know the right words."

I said, "I see it differently. When you say you can't help out, I think it may be more that you don't know how."

"What do you mean?"

"Well, you feel like an outsider, and I think that's not your fault, it's the church's. The church needs to know how to relate to the world, not the converse. Would you be interested in helping the outreach to the community? I think you have a lot to offer as to helping us connect with everyone."

My friend thought about it and agreed to meet with the outreach ministry at the church. He felt unqualified and had a lot of *I can't* thoughts, but he stepped up anyway. It was a great fit. He helped the church to learn what it is that unchurched people—which is most of the world—feel, think, and need. The *I can't* attitude never returned.

Where does *I can't* thinking come from? Often, people have had experiences in which they learned to fear risk and failure. Perhaps they tried a new sport or a class and failed miserably. Or perhaps they had significant relationships in which people close to them were critical and unaccepting of their failure. Sometimes these people simply learn that life is easier when you don't try, because when you avoid risk you don't hurt so much.

But *I can't* doesn't have to be part of your vocabulary. Failure can be your friend, because it's a great teacher. In fact, those people who succeed the most also fail the most. The research backs this up time and time again.

The Bible teaches the same thing about *I can't* thinking when it speaks about practicing those things which lead us to maturity: "But solid food is for the mature, who because of practice have their senses trained to discern good and evil" (Hebrews 5:14 NASB). Practicing means trying and failing, and practicing brings training to us. Practice is one of the antidotes to "I can't."

I can't is usually distorted thinking because it simply does not reflect reality. You can overcome the distortion by substituting reality phrases for *I can't* in your personal vocabulary. Here are a few that are usually more accurate than *I can't.*

I am avoiding difficulty: Trying to get that raise will be a lot of work; but it's more than I know to say whether I can or I can't before I try.

I am afraid: I fear that if I ask my friends to set me up with a date, they'll think I'm desperate.

I'm not sure: I can't tell what will happen when I tell my wife I'm not happy with our sex life, and it's hard for me to say things when I'm not sure about the outcome.

I won't: The catchall. I realize I really could start taking night courses for an MBA, but I just won't do it right now.

There is hope in all of these phrases, certainly a lot more than in the utterly hopeless "I can't!" If you label your excuses honestly, you can learn to face difficulties you are avoiding; your fears can be comforted and you can be reassured; a lack of sureness can turn to confidence; and even your refusal to make a move still implies that you have a choice. Whereas *I can't* takes the choice out of your hands. So pay attention to your vocabulary and banish *I can't* thinking (except maybe for your hope of playing in the NBA).

Distorted-Thinking Practice No. 1: Passive Language

Let's go back into your high school English class for a moment. Remember that verbs have voices, and voices can be active or passive, depending on what they are intended to convey. The active voice connotes that someone is doing something; the passive voice indicates that something is being done.

For example, if you say, "I quit my job," that is active. It means that you are the one who took the action to leave. If, however, you say, "I was laid off," you indicate an entirely different scenario. The passive voice of this phrase indicates that something beyond you is the reason you don't have the job (downsizing, economy, stock problems, or whatever). Whatever happened, it was not your fault. You are merely the passive recipient of the action.

Active and passive meanings have no moral value; they are neither good nor bad. They just convey different realities. But the problem comes when people use passive language to *explain their choices in such a way that they disown responsibility, ownership, and empowerment.* They have selected a way of thinking and communicating to others that hampers their ability to take charge and take action to get what they need.

Let's look at some examples of using passive language, and how it could be recast in ways more helpful in meeting your goals:

- *I was prevented from getting to the meeting on time by the traffic.*
  How about, "I chose to chat on the phone too long before I got in the car"?

- *The opportunity to bring up the problem didn't come up in the conversation.*
  How about, "I felt awkward, so I didn't say anything"?

- *He made me go to that horrible movie.*
  How about, "I gave him control over my choices"?

- *We ended up in bed.*
  How about, "I let my guard down and chose to have sex with him"?

- *I was manipulated into buying the stock.*
  How about, "I chose to not do the research myself, and gave the power and responsibility to that group"?

- *I'm waiting on God to find me the perfect job.* (This clothes irresponsible passivity—a passive attitude—in pseudo-spiritual language.) How about, "I don't want to send out resumes, call people, and go online. It's too much trouble"?

When you hold these passive excuses up to the light and expose them, they are not very pretty. And there are lots more examples of passive language than these few. But you get the point. It's all about learning to put yourself back on the hot seat, which is certainly uncomfortable, but when you compare that momentary discomfort to the reality that you are now back in the driver's seat of your life, it's worth it. Now you can get back to what *you* can do and achieve. Until you do that, other people are in charge of your life.

Distorted-Thinking Practice No. 2: Negative Thinking

The minds of some people seem to work negatively all the time on just about everything. Whatever the event, problem, or opportunity, they cast a dark light on it which discourages them and keeps them from the moves they need to make. For them, the glass is always half empty, and the light at the end of the tunnel is always a train.

Research indicates that negative thinkers will key in on three basic areas of life: themselves, the world, and the future. They see themselves as unlucky, even as losers who never get a break. They look at the world as unfriendly to them, oppressing their chances, and giving others more opportunity. They don't see their future as positive and hopeful. It seems bleak and dark, with no hope to brighten it up.

You may have tendencies toward negative thinking and not even be aware of them. You may think you are simply being realistic. You may even think, *Those positive thinkers are out of touch with reality. They live in the clouds and don't understand life the way it really is.*

You can see how negative thinking can paralyze your ability to combat the culture of blame and prevent you from taking hold of your life in an exciting and change-producing way. Taking chances, risks, and dreaming great dreams takes energy and passion. That energy and passion get sapped and drained when we are plagued by negative thinking. For example, suppose you want to improve your marriage, which is getting stale and humdrum. Maybe you'd like to recapture the intimacy and great feelings of your early days with your spouse.

But if you struggle with negative thinking, what do you come up against when you have these desires? You encounter thoughts like these: *It's too much work; I don't have it in me anymore* (myself—it's more than I can handle). *Besides, he won't respond. He never has, and he's happy with the way things are anyway* (the world—that's just the way things are). *Better that I just accept the way things are and get happiness in my work or the kids* (the future—nothing will ever get better). Can you imagine a more complete shutdown of the energy and passion you need to attain your dream?

However, remember what we said earlier about the way your thinker works: *just because you feel it or think it doesn't mean it's always true!* Have the courage to question your mind. It is saying *something*, but maybe not what it should. Look at the negative thoughts as a signal of a problem, not a statement of ultimate truth.

In fact, it's not true that a spouse cannot bring positive change to a marriage. People do this all the time. They sit down and talk to their mate. They recommit to their earlier love. They start becoming intentional about getting close and resolving alienations between them. They go off on weekends without the kids. They go to a marriage retreat with their church. They join a small group which specializes in rekindling marriage. As a psychologist, I have seen such steps as these make huge improvements in many marriages.[1]

What else could those negative thoughts mean? Several things. One could be a fear of risk and failure. Another could be hopelessness. Still another could be a passive outlook on life. Scratch the surface a little and try to understand why these thoughts are activated, and in what circumstances. We'll give you more steps to follow later in this chapter.

Sometimes depression is the cause of negative thoughts. When people suffer from depression, their minds often point away from the positive and spiral downward into hopelessness. Their depression is like an anchor, pulling all thoughts and emotions down into the dark. The person is not aware that his own mind is creating his dark view; to him it seems like reality.

For example, I was counseling a businessman who had depression. He was unhappy with his job and where he was in his career at this stage of life. The conversation went something like this:

"How could you improve your job position?" I asked.

"I can't. I've tried, and there's no room in the organization to move up."

"What about another job?"

"The industry is slow. That would be suicide."

"What about another industry?"

"That would be worse. Retraining at my age would be impossible."

"What about learning to be content where you are?"

"That doesn't work. It's not a fit for who I am."

At that point, I realized something: *I was not having a conversation with a man. I was talking to his depression.* His depression controlled the flow of the dialogue.

There is a very important principle to understand when dealing with depression. Depression *attaches itself to our circumstances.* Like glue, depression sticks to whatever events are in our lives, and it causes us to perceive them as negative. This man's depression attached itself to his work life, making him think that work was the problem. But it wasn't. In fact, we started paying more attention to the depression, and less to the job. As he began to see progress in his emotions, he began feeling more and more hopeful and positive. And as the depression began lifting, we started talking once again about his work. This time, it was very different:

"How could you improve your job position?"

"I've been thinking about that. I haven't really gone after a better position like I could have. Here are a couple of ideas that I want to try out with my boss."

And in time, he was promoted to a much better situation in his company.

Do you see what happened here? Same circumstances, but a very different outcome. The difference was that the depression, which had attached itself to his work like a leech to your leg, was removed, and his thinking became more positive and affirming.

Distorted-Thinking Practice No. 3: Defensive Thinking

Sometimes distorted thinking causes our minds to work against us. Strange as it seems, our minds will often work very hard to ward off thoughts of any positive plans, changes, and improvements. The mind will create a million excuses and defenses designed to keep us snug in our comfort zone and away from anxiety and tension. This is called defensive thinking. If you see this tendency in yourself, you need to resolve it and get past it, for it is another insidious dream-robber.

There are many of these defensive thinking patterns. We will show you four prominent ones that are particularly powerful in stopping our growth and goals. I call them the *Four Horsemen of Defense.*

The first horseman is *Denial*. When we face a particularly unpleasant or painful circumstance, our minds sometimes deny that it is true reality. We say to ourselves, *That can't be right; no way!* This is especially true when we need to look at our own part in failures or disappointments.

For example, when the school calls again about a son's misconduct, a parent might react with immediate denial: *My kid couldn't have done this; they must have the wrong boy.* Denial preserves us from the stress of tackling the appropriate problem solving that's needed. Reality thinking will take a more realistic and helpful approach, such as, *I need to meet with the principal and see what my son is doing and learn what I can do to help him straighten out. This will not be fun, but I must look at it as an opportunity to give him the chances he needs for success.*

The second horseman of defense is *Minimizing*. Not as serious as denial, but another dream-robber. Look at it as *denial-lite*. When we encounter problems or obstacles, our minds will look for ways to do damage control, so that we don't experience the full impact of the issue. A minimizing parent might respond to the phone call from the school in this way: *Sure, he gets wiggly; I know that. But I'm sure it's not as bad as the teacher said. She's overreacting.*

Minimizing helps anesthetize the discomfort of a problem. But it extracts a price: *you can only achieve success to the level that you accept and own the situation.* When you minimize, you guarantee that your son will not get all the help he needs; that your eating will never truly get under control; that your dream career will be limited; and so on. Minimizing must give way to a commitment to truth and reality, no matter how uncomfortable it is.

The third horseman is *Excusing*. When we call out this third pattern of defensive thinking, we may admit the reality, but we remove ourselves from any ownership of it. Excusing is not as serious as denial—at least we admit our kid has a school problem—but we handicap our chances to help him: *I know his conduct is poor in class. He's really bright, but the teacher doesn't understand him. So he gets bored, and he doesn't feel supported by her.* Do you see the shift of ownership and responsibility? Now the teacher needs to be inserviced on your son's personality type! Excusing your son's behavior in the present doesn't bode well for his future success. What happens when he is twenty-four years old and gets a bad report from his supervisor? You won't be there to say, "Obviously, you're not providing the stimulating work environment my son needs."

There are certainly legitimate excuses for some of the things that happen in life. But ask yourself, *When I face the challenge of reaching a goal or confronting a problem, do I automatically default to an excuse?* Excuses are also called "Yes-but" thinking. "Yes but I had bad traffic." "Yes but I'm too tired to research my dream job." "Yes but I've tried everything." If you find yourself excusing, get your "but" out of the way!

The fourth horseman is *Rationalizing.* This defense is what politicians are always accused of: presenting questionable behavior in the most favorable light possible. When you rationalize, you become your own spin doctor.

We all do it to a degree. *Certainly my kid acts out in class. He's a natural leader. That's so much better than his being just another sheep, blindly following the rules.* I kid you not, I have heard several parents use that spin to explain their aggressive, out-of-control children. Rationalizing problem behavior is a prime ingredient in the recipe for creating a long-term conduct problem that will one day make this boy's future wife miserable. You want to save your kid from that fate and help him be responsible, responsive, and self-controlled. But the only way to do that is to get rid of the spin and focus closely on what is true, even if that truth is dark. Your chances of success are much higher now than if you put it off.

People who use the Four Horsemen often are not aware that they are employing defensive patterns. The impulse of defensiveness is so ingrained that it seems a natural way to face problems. After all, such patterns of thinking protect us from unpleasant realities such as failure, struggle, and doubt. But if you don't deal with these realities head-on, they can stop your life path.

Don't be afraid to look at yourself honestly and critically. Be curious and question whether you have difficulty seeing yourself as you really are—as a person who may have problems, who may cause problems, or who may be failing. It may not be a pretty sight, but if it's true, you need to know it. It's much better to know the truth than to preserve your comfort with an illusion that keeps you stuck in unreality. When you quit putting up defenses against the truth, you enable yourself to take charge of your own world.

At this point we have shown what distorted thinking can do to our minds. Sometimes it causes them to be so negative they discourage our ownership and risk-taking. At other times, distorted thinking can cause our minds to be so unrealistically positive that they protect us from culpability and accountability. Sometimes they do both at the same time. However, there are very workable solutions to negative thinking that will make a positive difference in the way you live your life.

Steps to Thinking Better

You need your mind.

To reach your potential, to achieve your goals and dreams, whether they be about career, love, family, habits, or spiritual growth, you need your mind to be your ally and friend, not an obstacle. A mind plagued with excuses, negativity, passive discouragement, and similar contamination is like an engine full of sludge. It will not get you where you want to go.

So we want to show you some of the best steps you can take to revive your thinker and make it help rather than hinder your efforts to be more successful.

Step No. 1: Commit Yourself to Raw Reality

Reality may not be pleasant, but no problem was ever solved, no goal ever reached without looking at the situation squarely with no editing or reframing. Don't be afraid to say, *I need to know what is true, not what I hope is true.* That is your sure path. Look for raw, unvarnished reality, not the prepackaged, politically acceptable type.

Suppose you had extensive diagnostic testing, and the tests showed clearly that you need heart bypass surgery. That's a big deal. You see your doctor for his recommendation, and he says, "The surgery route just seems so serious and harsh. Why don't you take a couple of aspirin and get a good night's sleep instead?" The good doctor is trying to save you from discomfort. The simple prescription he offers is certainly a very pleasant alternative to surgery, but there are two major problems with it: *It wouldn't address the true reality. And it wouldn't get you the outcome you wanted.*

Remember that accepting reality is like a reset button for rebooting your computer. It gives you a fresh start. When facing any problem or goal, always ask yourself, *What is real and true here? What is my thinking missing that I need to know?*

On the other hand, suppose you struggle with the negative *I can't* or *I've tried everything* thinking. You often find yourself unable to feel the courage to make your moves. The appeal to reality applies here as well. Commit yourself to seeing the real situation for what it is, *including what you can do about it.* Develop the habit of thinking along lines similar to the following:

- I'll talk to someone and brainstorm to see if I've looked at every angle.

- Maybe I've given too much power to another person in my life, and I need to take it back.

- So what if I try this and screw up? Currently, Derek Jeter gets out 70 percent of the time and he does okay. The reality is that failure doesn't end everything.

- The problem may not be that *I can't*; it may be that *I won't*, for some reason. I need to find out which it is.

- If I keep waiting for someone or something to change, I may be waiting a long time.

- Before I give up, I will make a good plan and stick to it longer than I ever have before.

Reality will never fail you. It is how God sees everything, and he uses reality to accomplish his purposes. In fact, reality and truth are part of his own makeup. He is "full of unfailing love and truth" (Psalm 86:15 NLT). Seek reality and you will find God there, helping your thoughts conform to the truth.

Step No. 2: Become a Humble Person

Humility is a trait of greatness. It is not an aspect of timid people who see themselves as trash. Humility is the ability to *see yourself and your situation clearly, for good and for bad.* Humble people don't care if what they do or think makes them look like a hero or a bad guy. They want to get at the heart of the matter.

I had a friend, similar to the one Henry talks about in the previous chapter, controlled by negative thinking patterns that kept him from asking out a woman he was attracted to. He said, "She wouldn't go for a guy like me; she's a total goddess and I'm pretty mediocre." After a few attempts to encourage him, I realized my folly. I realized I was heading the wrong direction, and said, "Actually, in a way, that could be a pride issue for you."

"What?" he said, not expecting that kind of reaction. "I thought you were saying I put myself down too much."

"I did, but sometimes pride can drive our self-talk too."

"What do you mean?"

"Well, let's look at it. How prideful is it to think that your mediocrity is so unattractive that you don't have a chance? That actually gives a lot of power to your unattractive self-image. In fact, think about how you're not even giving this gal a chance to choose you. That could even be seen as controlling."

He had never thought about it that way. He realized that he wasn't being truly humble—that is, seeing himself clearly. He finally asked her out and she accepted! So give up the idea that your past, your problems, and your limitations are all that powerful. Be humble enough to allow for the possibility that you can do better—and then act on that possibility.

Step No. 3: Be a Self-Observer

Develop the ability to monitor yourself. Observe what you do, why you do it, and when you do it. As Dr. Howard Hendricks, one of my favorite professors, used to say, "Become a student of yourself." That is a trait of successful people, and they achieve success because they are able to confront the truth about themselves and get over their inaccurate and unhelpful thinking patterns.

When I consult with people who come to me with problems, I often have them try this exercise. "Imagine that you are in two places at once: one 'you' is in a real interaction with someone else, discussing some goal or problem. The second 'you' is floating above, near the ceiling, looking at the interaction of the other you and learning from it. After you leave the conversation, you can use that floating, observing 'you' to review what happened and consider what you could have done differently."

By employing this exercise you may learn that you give up power and choice very easily when someone has an objection to your idea. Or that you come down on yourself quickly when you are confronted. Or that you go into blame and excuses when you face a problem.

Such information is pure gold! Rooting out the truth about yourself may not be fun, but it will reap great rewards for you, for it allows you to see and own what you need to do and change. Without this ability, people are forced to interpret every bump in the road as fate, bad luck, or bad people. Nothing is their own fault. They are then rendered helpless and hopeless because it's all beyond their control. But the self-observant person who takes ownership of his future is way ahead of the pack.

Step No. 4: Forgive

At first blush, forgiveness may not seem to have anything to do with changing your thinking patterns. But it is highly critical to the process. When we forgive, we cancel a debt. That is the meaning of the word in the New Testament. In other words, we let go of our right to extract punishment, justice, and revenge from an offending person.

This releasing of negative baggage has great power to help us think more clearly, for unforgiveness clouds our minds with thoughts of victimization, powerlessness, punishment, unfairness, and retribution. When we haven't forgiven another person, we can't look at our situation or see our choices or see our own part in the problem. We focus only on what the other has done and what has been done to us. Forgiveness unlocks the key to that prison, enabling us to flush out the hurt and obsessions about the offending person. Then our minds can once again be clear to think about hope, action, dreams, and goals.

Step No. 5: Create and Write Down the Good Slogans

Your mind has been coming up with excuses to keep you from owning your future, and it has probably been doing so for a long time. As you become more self-aware, start identifying the slogans you have been repeating to yourself that have been chaining you down. We all have them. But go further than that and create new slogans that counter the bad ones. Craft these new slogans so that they put the true vision into perspective.

Write these new slogans down and keep them around you in places that will remind you of what is true and real. Put them in the screensaver on your computer. Place sticky notes on your bathroom mirror and refrigerator. When negative thoughts invade your mind, look at these notes. When you are doing okay, look at them anyway to keep yourself centered on reality. When you are doing the cognitive work of training your mind, the personal work of embracing reality, and being humble and forgiving, the presence of these new slogans can be powerful and effective. Here are a few examples:

- No more *I can't* excuses. *I can*, and *I will.*

- When I fail, I will learn from it and move on.

- I will not wait for life to find me. I will find life.

- There is great opportunity for a great future.

- I am the only person who can own my dreams, and I choose to own them.

- Blame will not get me where I want to go. Ownership will get me there.

- When I take responsibility for my problems, I am in charge.

Rotate your slogans. Come up with fresh ones every few weeks. Put them in different places. Keep it interesting. Don't let sameness cause you to ignore and forget about them. God understands the power of writing and repetition to help us remember, and that is why he encouraged his people to use this method centuries ago. He wants us to know, remember, and experience the realities that bring about success.

Look at what he told his people after he gave them his law:

> These words, which I am commanding you today, shall be on your heart. You shall teach them diligently to your sons and shall

talk of them when you sit in your house and when you walk by the way and when you lie down and when you rise up. You shall bind them as a sign on your hand and they shall be as frontals on your forehead. You shall write them on the doorposts of your house and on your gates. (Deuteronomy 6:6–9 NASB)

Remember the Ambrose Bierce quote at the beginning of this chapter: "Brain: An apparatus with which we think we think." Bierce was trying to be funny, but he was also being cynical. The reality is that God gave you a brain, not as an apparatus to make you think that you think, but as a tool to help you to see reality for what it is, and then to think, plan, dream, and take ownership of your life. You can own your own thinker! Take charge of it.

3

You Can Always Find a Choice

3

I remember the meeting as if it were yesterday, probably because the dynamic that almost derailed the discussion is one of my pet peeves.

I was serving as a consultant in a planning retreat with a business group that was constructing a strategic plan. The company was rich with open opportunities, and it was poised to accomplish a lot of exciting things. Several of us saw the possibilities as endless, and we were really excited about the potential.

"Let's do this," I said, and then I explained an idea sure to bring about expansion and profit. "The result could be incredible!"

"Well, that would be nice," said one of the chief team members. "But we don't have the resources for that."

"So?" I said. "What does that have to do with anything?"

"Well," she retorted, "It's a wonderful plan, but we really can't entertain that option. To pull a thing like that off will take a lot of people and a lot of money—resources that we don't have."

"Yes," I said. "I understand that you don't have them. I still don't get what that has to do with anything."

"What do you mean?" she said. "If you don't have the resources, you simply can't do it. I don't understand what you don't get."

"Not having the resources does not mean you can't do it," I said. "You still have choices."

"I know," she said. "But this option is not one of them."

"I must disagree," I replied. "You are forgetting something. You have lots of choices other than just saying no to this opportunity. You have the choice, for example, to go out and find the resources—the money and the people that you don't have."

"How would we do that?" she asked.

"I don't know yet," I said. "We'll have to look into it. You could find partners, investors, or strategic alliances that would benefit from the outcome and have them put money and people into it. You could sell the idea to someone bigger and then have a piece of it. You could build the plan out slowly from the place where we are, and then when it's up and running, find the investment. You could find another group who needs this piece in their puzzle and piggy-back with them. Who knows until we get into it? But, you certainly have choices."

But clearly the dream-killer was still not on board, and I began to get a little frustrated. "Or, you could dye your hair orange, move to Colorado, and sell popsicles while you spin around in circles and sing 'Three Blind Mice,'" I said.

"What?" she asked. She looked befuddled and irritated at me.

"My point is this," I said. "You have tons of choices available to you, including the last one and a million others. Unlimited choices. If you open your eyes to those choices, you can make this thing work and get where you want to go. But if the first roadblock you hit makes you think it's all over—as if you have no choices—you will never get anywhere."

We then got into a valuable discussion that changed the mindset of the entire company. The group began to look at possibilities in different ways. They began to see options, opportunities, and solutions that they never would have seen before. And it led to positive results, both in that particular situation and others as well.

Those results came from a particular shift in the way they saw the world and themselves. The shift was this:

From *I don't have a choice,* to *I may not have the choice I want, but I can find other choices instead.*

Almost every day Dr. Townsend and I see people who hit a situation and feel helpless to correct it because they think they have no choice. Here are a few common examples:

- I have talked to my husband, but he just won't listen.

- I have tried to get dates, but there are just no good ones out there.

- I tried counseling, but it did not help me.

- I tried a weight-loss program, but it didn't work.

- I confronted my friend, but she would not listen.

- I tried talking to my mother, but she just got angry.

- I want a new career, but they aren't hiring new positions at my company.

The common denominator in all these complaints points back to our theme of ownership. Each of these statements is saying, "It's not my fault; it's someone else or the circumstance. So there's nothing I can do." Okay, you do not have the circumstance you want. You did not get the answer you wanted. The critical question is, who *owns* that result? In this list, the owners of the result are:

- The husband

- The dating environment

- The last counselor who was not helpful

- The weight-loss group

- The friend

- The mother

- The company

But, none of *those* people is out there worrying, suffering, or fretting about the result. Only the people passing the buck are feeling the results. That's where the result lives—in the complainers' lives and souls. For them to take ownership would mean that they must recognize that the problem always ends up at the doorstep of the one who is responsible for correcting it. The problem may not be their fault, but they are the ones bearing the results—who really own the results—for they have to live with them. It is their problem, not the problem of those other people. This means they are the ones *responsible* for doing something about it. It's up to them to find what choices are available to them that they are not yet seeing.

If you are the wife of the husband who won't listen, and you want him to "get it," what are your choices? You have more than you can imagine. And many of them, if you take ownership and responsibility, have a good chance of getting him to change. Others will result in your being happy even if he does not change. Either way, you have choices. You are not relegated to a miserable life because your husband (or wife) is not listening to you about some problem. What are some of your choices? You can:

- Ask someone to evaluate the effectiveness of the way you're communicating the problem to him. Something in your approach may be contributing to the problem.

- Tell him that in spite of your efforts to communicate, he is not hearing you, and you want to discuss why he is not responding and determine how the two of you can find a solution.

- Tell him that if he does not get it, there are going to be some consequences.

- Tell him that you want him to go with you to counseling.

- Tell him that if he doesn't join you in counseling, there are going to be consequences.

- Tell him that if he doesn't join you in counseling, you will go alone to see what your options are.

- Figure out who has leverage with him—someone he will listen to—and get that person to talk to him with you.

- Do an intervention.

- Unplug from your need for him to get it, thus cutting off his power over your emotional wellbeing.

- Join an outside support system to get what you need in terms of connectedness, support, validation, and so on.

- Work through your issues from the past that his patterns tap into to fuel your pain.

- Become so strong that he has no more ability to make you react. Then shower him with love, leaving him speechless with no one to fight and blame for his life.

These are only a few of the scads of options available. *You are never without options.* That is the nature of God's creation. Yes, we are dealt a certain hand of cards, but we choose how to play them. A good player can win even with a bad hand. God has given you a creative will, and he gives you open doors to find a way out of any situation. Listen to the words of Solomon (Proverbs 11:9 NIV): With his mouth the godless destroys his neighbor, but *through knowledge the righteous escape.*

Or the words of Paul:

> No temptation has seized you except what is common to man. And God is faithful; he will not let you be tempted beyond what you can bear. But when you are tempted, *he will also provide a way out so that you can stand up under it.* (1 Corinthians 10:13 NIV, emphasis added)

God promises that there is no such thing as "no way out." When we seek God, he will provide some way to escape whatever it is that ensnares us. We often see that reality in people whose lives are working. No matter what happens to them, they find a way out. In other words:

Their circumstances do not have control of them. They always find choices.

As they look for God and his answers and search for the options, one always appears. A choice is there. It may not be the one they wanted, but there is always a viable option available.

So, why don't we always see it?

First, it may be that we are not open to it. We want the option we want, and if that option is not available, then we often get stuck in blame and protest loudly that, "It's not my fault." I think this is the main reason a lot of people remain stuck. They know what they want, and when that's not an option, they think there are no options. It may be due to stubbornness, or it may just be an overinvestment in their preferred option.

This scenario often occurs in relationships. Some people never get over a relationship not working. I have a friend whose parents divorced thirty years ago when she was in high school. I ran into her recently and asked about them.

"Dad is doing well," she replied. "He is remarried and really happy. He found a very nice woman and seems to have grown a lot since you knew him. I am really happy for him."

"How about your mom?" I asked.

"Not so good," she said. "She just stayed stuck after the divorce. She's still hung up on my dad and wants him back. She is seventy now and quite bitter. It is not any fun to be around her. The family avoids her."

Her story saddened me. I remember her mother. Vibrant and full of personality, outgoing and beautiful, she would have been quite the catch for someone. But apparently she would not open her eyes to other options available if she could not have the one she wanted. If not her former husband, she would consider no one else.

Why? Who knows? I don't know the woman well enough to speculate, because I don't know what all is going through her head. But whatever the reason driving her refusal to consider options, the result is the same: she is stuck in her miserable condition. And the hard truth is that it's her own fault. She simply did not open herself to the options available to her when the one she desired was closed off.

Adaptability

One of the most important qualities that a person can have is the ability to adapt. It is one of the measuring sticks that psychologists use to determine a person's maturity and mental health. Adaptability is one of the strengths that vaults a person into adulthood. Think about it. When children cannot get a particular need met—such as hunger—they look to Mommy or Daddy to find the solution. Maybe it's a nice dinner of hot dogs. But when the children are grown, there is no Mommy or Daddy to come up with another option for dinner if all the hot dogs are gone. The mature person is on his own to find a way to adapt to that reality.

But what if you are not adaptable? You look in the fridge and find that there are no wieners. Being unwilling to adapt and look at options, you say, "Well, no dinner for me tonight." So you go to bed hungry. And bitter at the world.

But if you are adaptable, you will adjust your expectations and say, "I have choices." You will begin to ask yourself questions: "What if I call my neighbor and ask if he has a few spare frankfurters?" "What if I look up a good take-out service?" "How about going out and finding an open food store or a late-night restaurant?" You realize that you have choices other than just sitting there and going hungry.

Of course, most people would easily see their options when dealing with the minor inconvenience of hot dog deprivation. But people do fail every day in the same simple process of adaptation when dealing with relationship struggles, emotional difficulties, career stumbling blocks, and the like. They hit the obstacle and think they have no choice but to live with the problem. But if they are open to other choices, a viable option always shows up.

Learned Helplessness

Another obstacle to finding one's options is what psychologists call "learned helplessness." The term comes from some original experiments in which animals were put in situations where no choice available to them would lead to a good outcome. Soon the animals learned to think that no matter what they did, nothing good would come of it. There was nothing they could do to improve their lot. They were truly helpless to change their fate, so they simply gave up and quit trying. When these animals determined that they were helpless, or better put, powerless, they would just endure their hopeless condition *even when a visible escape was provided them.* They would not take the escape route because their belief system told them that they had no good choice, even when they were staring it right in the face.

People do the same thing. They develop "learned helplessness," and it is actually a formula for depression. They learn early in life that no matter what they do, it will not affect the outcome whatsoever. No matter what they do, Dad or Mom can't be pleased. No matter what they do, someone still gets angry. No matter what they do, they do not get the approval that they need. No matter what they do, they cannot escape the bad outcome. It's just the way it is. So they quit trying.

Then something even worse happens. In addition to giving up on trying, *they develop a way of seeing themselves as powerless in relation to the world.* They no longer see the world as operating on a cause-and-effect model in which one's actions produce a corresponding result. Instead, they come to see it operating on a random model in which things just happen and there is little you can do about them. The law of sowing and reaping goes out the window. So they quit sowing into their lives, and as a result, they also quit reaping. Why? Because they believe that there are no choices. Nothing they do can make things better, so when nothing happens to make things better, it is never their fault.

Apply that way of thinking to the situations we listed above and you can see how some people stay stuck in their bad situations for many years. Let's look at their list of excuses again:

- The husband who wouldn't listen

- The poor dating environment

- The counselor who didn't help

- The weight-loss program that didn't work

- The friend who wouldn't listen

- The mother who got angry

- The company that wasn't hiring

But the reality is—and I can tell you this with all certainty—that every single day, other people in those same situations do not just accept them as they are and resign themselves to misery. Instead, they believe that there are always choices, and they join the hand of God to find a way out of the captivity of their situation. They look past the choice they wish they could have and search for the one that works. And they find it.

What It Looks Like

Sometimes seeing a way of thinking in action helps you to adopt it as your own. Many people grow up in situations where looking for choices was not modeled to them, and they don't even know what the process looks like. (They are not the ones you want on your scavenger hunt team, by the way.) But if they could see "choice discovering" modeled for them, they could learn it. So let's look at choice discovering modeled in a few specific situations in order to learn the choices always available to us. These examples involving dating, emotional issues, and weight loss will help you picture how expanding your options means you never really hit a dead-end.

Choice-Discovering Model: Dating

I was speaking to singles in the Los Angeles area about dating when a woman raised her hand and said, "I hear all of this stuff about dating, but it's very difficult to find anyone good to date in a place like L.A. The people are so transient . . . no one seems to have any roots here, so they just come and go. As a result, there are no real stable communities where everyone knows each other and can help connect you with someone compatible."

I could not believe my ears. Southern California has about twenty million people. And she thinks there are no dating options in that pool?

It was the classic externalization of the problem we've been discussing. Her inability to find good dating material was not her fault; it was the environment. "Southern California offers no good choice of men. So I'm stuck; there is nothing I can do."

The real kicker was in the next thing she said: "It would be a lot easier to find good dates in the Midwest, where people and communities are much more stable."

Why was that such a significant statement? Because earlier that very week, I had been in the Midwest talking to singles and a woman had said, "It is so difficult to find anyone to date here in the Midwest. People have been here so long and the communities are so established that everyone knows each other already and you can't break into the circle. So there are no new prospects." And then she said, of all things, *"It would be so much easier to find people to date in a place like L.A. or New York."*

Suffice it to say that I was well equipped to refute California Girl's excuse. What was keeping these women from finding the dates they desired? One thing: not seeing the fact that they had choices. Their geography was their excuse. It prevented them from finding the relationships they wanted. Their thought process went like this: "I am not getting what I want. Guess that is the way it is around here." Translated into our earlier metaphor, "There are no hot dogs in this fridge, so I guess there's no dinner tonight."

But, the true reality is quite different than their perceived reality. I met and talked with singles in both locales who were finding very fulfilling dating lives right where those two women said it was impossible. Just like our two complainers, these dating women had also experienced "datelessness." But instead of burying their dreams in a tear-soaked handkerchief, they asked themselves, "What are the choices I could make to change this situation?" There were only about a million, but here are a few that these women saw and activated:

- Some looked at themselves and figured out the fact that they were not getting dates because of something out of kilter about themselves. So they asked their friends for feedback about themselves, and when they got it, they went to work on the problem. When they corrected it, their dating lives changed. The things they corrected ranged all the way from "you are not open to different kinds of men other than your own dream ideal," to "you don't come across as open to men in social situations." Some of these women got in better shape; others had to address certain internal attitudes that were keeping them stuck.[1]

- Some of these women figured out that they were not getting dates because they were not meeting enough people. So they joined a dating service. I just got a phone call from a woman who had told me a little over a year ago that "there were no good men to date," and that "she never got asked out." At that time I challenged her to work my program of dating that urges participants to stop blaming outside circumstances and start seeing their choices. I urged her to join a dating service, but she was resistant; she did not at first see that as a viable choice. But in time her attitude changed and she became open to her choices. Well, I'll cut to the chase and tell you why she called me. She had just said yes to a marriage proposal from a great guy who came from one of those dating services. And, as she would tell you, he was not the first man she met. She had to choose to continue her search after the first ones did not work out. (See chapter 8 on persisting.)

- These women figured out that their "traffic pattern" was not exposing them to people they had never met before. They realized that there was no one magic bullet—no single place where everyone found dates. So they expanded their range and started going to new places.

- The women also got active when there were no good activities available where they could meet other singles. They began to organize activities on their own. One group of women from my church started a club called S.W.A.R.M., which stands for "Single Women Actively Recruiting Men." They organized monthly gatherings and outings to which members invited men they were not attached to but had met through work or some other venue. In essence, they were all recruiting for each other.

The list could go on, but the point is, whatever problem they found in themselves, they corrected it and their date life turned around.

The point here is not in the specific suggestions, although many of them are highly creative and effective. The point is *the way of thinking that led to those suggestions*. These women realized that when something is not working, stop blaming. Stop passively complaining, "It's not my fault" and get busy figuring out what your choices are. When you don't see any choices, keep looking or create them on your own.

Choice-Discovering Model: Emotional Issues

The caller on our radio show asked what she could do about her eating disorder. She had suffered from bulimia for quite a while. She told us that she was in a 12-step program that had helped her in some ways, but it had left her bulimia largely untouched. Her counselors had convinced her that her bulimia was an addiction and that she would always be in recovery for it. But her recovery program was not helping, and she felt stuck.

"First," I said, "I have a big problem with calling bulimia an addiction. In my way of thinking, an addiction is something that involves a substance that you can't let go of, and it involves such factors as acquired tolerance, withdrawal effects, and a whole list of other things not associated with your problem. While the term *addiction* may be a helpful metaphor for some out-of-control behaviors, I do not think that the addiction model of treatment is the answer for bulimia."

"But it does involve a substance," she said. "Food."

"I understand," I told her, "but the difference in food and alcohol, for example, is that you will always eat food, even after you are no longer bulimic. Alcoholics should never touch alcohol again. Their body has acquired an addiction reaction that will always trigger a downslide to non-functional status. There is no safe way for them ever to drink again. There is a good way for you to eat. So, don't limit yourself to a treatment that is successful for addicts but does not address the issues that are driving your bulimia."

"What do you mean?" she asked.

"Bulimia is usually driven by some predictable developmental issue," I replied, "like need-fear dilemmas, autonomy struggles involving boundaries and freedom, perfectionism and ideal demands, and a failure to achieve adulthood in relation to symbolic parent figures. If you would find a good therapist who understood those things, you could work through what is driving your bulimia, and then you would not have to live forever in 'recovery' for it. It would be gone. I have seen it happen a zillion times."

"But I tried counseling, and it didn't work," she said. That comment made me suspect the real issue behind the problems, but I probed further.

She went on to tell me all the issues that her counselor had addressed, and they were not the kinds of things that resolve bulimia. I told her she needed to find a new counselor, one who understands the kinds of issues that cause and maintain bulimia.

I could tell that she was struggling to believe that anything would really work. I could hear in her voice that she really had tried, and that the very thought of trying again was overwhelming her.

And here was the reason, as I suspected: She was not afraid of the effort of trying; she was afraid of trying and having it not work again. She was afraid of the hopelessness that would weigh down her heart if another attempt yielded no results. She knew well the danger of Proverbs 13:12, which says, "hope deferred makes the heart sick, but a longing fulfilled is a tree of life" (NIV).

But here is the point: *her hopelessness did not come from a course of action being tried and not working. It came from her way of thinking about trying.*

Think of it this way. This caller's philosophy was that you try something, hoping it will work, and if it doesn't you have no other options and everything is hopeless. No wonder this woman was holding back. Of course it would be a very scary thing to try anything. If I thought I had just one bullet, I wouldn't fire it until I had to. One shot is all you get, and after that it is Hopeless City. But—

What if your hope is not in any particular option; your hope is in the belief that if you keep looking for options, one will appear?

This approach makes a huge difference. *Huge!* If your hope is based in the fact that you always have choices instead of being vested solely in any one choice, then *you always have hope.* Hope need never end, because no matter how many disappointments or failures, you always look for the next available choice. When something does not work out, you immediately ask yourself, "What are my choices?" By considering your choices, you find that you always have somewhere to go other than into hopelessness. You have options, freedom, possibilities, and hope.

This caller had hit a wall because she saw no choices. Her 12-step program, though helpful in many ways, was not making her bulimia go away. (By the way, we are big supporters of 12-step programs. The point we are making here is that there are things that bulimics need to do in addition to 12-step work.) But as I pointed out to this woman, she had a lot of choices that she was not seeing. Here are just a few that we gave her in that short phone call:

- She could go back to counseling, but find a counselor who knows the developmental issues underlying bulimia. If the first one she talked to doesn't know them, then she should look for another.

- She could choose to bring other people into her struggle when it was actually happening. A 12-step program usually teaches people to call their sponsors or someone else who can help in the moment when the temptation is occurring. This woman could find help in calling someone when she was tempted to binge.

- If one meeting a week was not doing the job, she could choose to up the number of meetings until she got more control. I shared with her that sometimes when people are binging as often as she was, they choose to attend a meeting every day.

The co-host of our radio show, Steve Arterburn, shared with her that many alcoholics go to as many as ninety meetings in thirty days to get in control of their drinking.

- She could choose to admit to her sponsor and the people in her group the reality of where she really was in her struggle. She admitted that it was extremely hard for her to admit her need of other people. She had a choice about whether to admit that need and let others in on her failure when she was not exercising. Making that one choice to depend on others would go a long way in overcoming her bulimia, because bulimia usually involves dependency fears and conflicts.

- She could choose to get a good book[2] that addresses the issues behind bulimia. She could also choose to get into a small group of friends or find an accountability partner to help her work on her issues.

- She could find a specific support group on bulimia in her town and join it to learn what others are doing to overcome the problem.

- She could choose to go into a more structured treatment, like many bulimics do. Once-a-week counseling or a 12-step group is often not enough. She could check into a treatment center and stay awhile. This kind of treatment can be very successful.

Note that all this information was packed into a very short phone call. If someone were to sit down and spend time with this woman, I am sure that they would discover many other choices available to her as well. The point is this: *you always have choices.* If you do not have a terminal illness that is going to take your life in the next hour, you usually have options available to you. (As a matter of fact, the research shows that even in terminal illnesses people have many options which will drastically affect their quality and quantity of life.) Choices, choices, choices. We never run out of them.

However, we get stuck in our problems because of two things we don't like.

First, we don't like it when the choice we desire is not available to us. Consider the woman who was stuck at age seventy after getting divorced at forty because she still wanted her ex-husband. That option was not available and she would not entertain the other choices open to her. Meanwhile, her husband did make other choices and put together a good life for himself.

The second thing we often don't like is this: if the option we *have* chosen is not working, as in the case of the bulimic woman, we often don't want to look past it even though it is not yielding results. She was choosing her once-a-week 12-step program, and it was not working. But she wanted that option to work; she did not want to go through the hassle, the risk, and the dread of starting over. The axiom, *If you keep doing the same thing, you'll keep getting the same results*, applies to her way of thinking.

We have a tendency either to want our first choice that we can't have, or to cling to the failing one we have chosen. Neither option is viable, but that does not mean it is all over.

In dealing with emotional issues, there are always choices available that we might not be exercising. When your relationships are not working, you are not limited to patterns you have relied on in the past. You can stop doing what you have been doing and try something different. When it comes to emotional issues, people tend to limit themselves to their long-standing patterns of behaving.

I have a friend who has dealt with depression. When she is depressed her natural inclination is to stay in bed or withdraw. But she has the kind of character that understands choices and options. So when she is depressed she makes the choice to get up and go work out, no matter how she feels. And she makes the choice to call a friend, or go to a group, or get out with someone she is close to, no matter how she feels. She would tell you that these choices have made a huge difference at some very difficult times. While they are not the total cure, and she still has to make other hard choices in order to get well, exercising choices to be proactive about her condition has played a big part in improving it.

Look at your patterns of dealing with your emotional issues and then explore all the other choices available to you.

Another example: If you are plagued by feelings of loneliness, and yet you just go home and watch TV, it's time to make some choices to improve your condition. What other things could you do when you feel lonely? You could:

- Call a friend.

- Go to a church gathering.

- Join a small group or Bible study.

- Attend a generic recovery meeting and talk about loneliness.

- Do volunteer work.

- Take a class that meets at the times when you are most prone to loneliness.

- Mentor a child.

- Go exercise with a friend, or a class.

- One million other options not listed here.

The same principle applies to other emotional issues. Often people do not see options available to them other than the patterns they have always lived out. People with anger issues, for example, do not see that their first choice, which might be to never lose their temper, is not an option yet. Their anger does not just go away because they want it to. But they still have choices. They could choose to remove themselves from a situation when they feel their anger beginning to rise. They could learn to recognize the anger triggers and avoid them. Or when they first feel anger rising, they could tell the person affected that it is happening, and they need to back away from the situation.

As the Bible says, God will provide a way of escape.

Choice-Discovering Model: Weight Loss

"I tried the weight-loss group, and it didn't work." We hear this comment often on the radio show or in seminars. Or sometimes, "It worked for a while, but then I gained it all back." The despair that often accompanies this issue is heartbreaking, especially when people have "tried." But, when you begin to get below the surface, you often find that the problem was not the program that did not work, but the person who did not work the program. And that issue is related to not seeing available choices.

When looking at weight loss, people usually see two choices: eat less, and exercise more. And they are right. All the many research studies say the same thing: to lose weight, one needs to move about more and eat less. But there is a problem with that solution: people are unable to do it, or at least to sustain it. What they will do is join a program and sometimes get initial results. Then they gradually begin to wane in their commitment to the program. They begin to try just sticking to the diet, for example, instead of continuing in the groups as well. And soon they find what they have always found—that their willpower fails them. Their conclusion: "That didn't work for me."

In reality, what has not worked is often their openness to explore other choices. A number of key choices are available to anyone who is serious about getting control of an out-of-control behavior—choices that actually work. As it relates to our current discussion of weight loss, the lesson is this: when your willpower is failing, relying on the ineffective "don't eat that" is not your only choice. You could:

- *Add structure to your program.* If you are not able to stick to some program requirement, then you need more discipline from the outside. Example: A group of women that I know were having difficulty making the tough choices necessary to carry out their goal. So they made another choice. They chose something they *could* do. They chose to have a thirty-minute conference call every morning at 7:00 to go over what they had to do that day to make it work and support each other. That one choice made it all come together for them.

- *Choose to eliminate temptation.* If choosing to not eat the potato chips in the pantry is not a viable option because you lack the power to resist them, you can choose to not buy them in the first place. If they are not in the house, you are not going to eat them. People find this technique extremely helpful. They choose to not have any of the no-no foods in the house.

- *Choose external self-control support.* If you cannot follow the above suggestion because you can't pass by potato chips in the grocery store, then don't go shopping alone. Shop with a friend who is in the program with you, or with someone committed to your goal. If you are alone and feeling tempted, have a few friends whom you have agreed to call at such moments to talk you through it. Tell them that you are about to get into trouble and you want help. Make the choice to promise them that you will never cheat without calling them first.

- *Choose to bring external discipline and structure to the specific tasks.* If you are supposed to exercise several times a week, and you cannot do it because of your lack of self-control, borrow someone else's structure. Choose to join a class, or choose to assemble a group of friends who will meet every morning, or at lunchtime, and walk or work out together. You may not have the willpower to do it on your own, but you can join others and tap into their willpower. College students utilize this option all the time by joining study groups to help them get done what they lack the discipline to do on their own. Hiring a trainer accomplishes the same thing.

- *Choose to deal with the emotions and stresses that are driving you to eat.* While willpower is not one of your choices, talking to someone about the problems that may cause your overeating is one possible option. Join a group, see a counselor, meet with a friend, and begin to get at what's eating you. Journaling is helpful for some people. You always have a choice to let your emotions either be yours alone, or to share them with someone else. When you share them, they will become less powerful, and they will lose the ability to drive you to the behavior over which you have lost control.

- *Choose to not drop out of your program.* Over and over again we hear of people who have joined a particular program, achieved some success, but then dropped out. Not only did they gain back the weight they lost, which, as the research shows, usually happens, more often than not they gained even more. Then they say, "I tried that and it did not work for me." But in most cases, it was the dropping out that caused it to not work.

If you are truly interested in success, you must make two choices here. First, you must choose not to drop out of the program, even if you are not happy with the initial results. The ones who continue are the ones who end up getting good results. Second, choose to do something that will help you to stay in the program. Usually that means getting the kind of outside support and accountability mentioned above. Staying in the program is the most powerful choice. Forget the choice of relying on your willpower to keep from overeating. Don't cling to a choice doomed to failure.

- *Choose to see weight loss as a long-term lifestyle change.* Getting into this kind of continuing-the-program mindset is the most important choice you can make. Weight loss is not something you simply "do." It is a matter of changing your lifestyle to where it's the same as the people who do not have weight problems. Those slim and trim people do the same things as the people who are trying to lose weight. They explore their emotions, seek support, avail themselves of the same kinds of structured exercise routines, and so on. Ever think about that? It's the skinny people you see at the gym. They go routinely; it's their way of life. And that is the way you must choose to see your weight-control routine. It is not a choice just to lose weight. It is a much more far-reaching choice: the choice to change your lifestyle. When you do that, the weight-control choices will begin to take care of themselves.

This brief discussion is certainly not meant to be a weight-loss guide or a comprehensive program. We have counseled too many people with weight issues to think we can offer a cure-all in a few pages. If weight is your problem, our hearts go out to you, and we encourage you to find good help with a reputable program that shows proven results. But remember, the good programs work only if you work the program. Choose to find one that you can continue to work, or choose to get the support structures that you will need to keep working it. That will be the key to your success.

CIRCLES OF CHOICE

Remember the section on adaptability? We noted that a child who has no dinner has no choice in the matter, as he or she is dependent on a caretaker for everything. But an adult with an empty refrigerator has choices. Then we said something else very important for you to remember.

We pointed out that most of you do not lose sight of your choices in a simple situation like no food in the fridge. You easily see that you have other options, like heading for the supermarket, going to a restaurant, or moseying over to your neighbor's house to make a sandwich. No problem. But when you hit a relational roadblock or a work roadblock, the "I have no choice" thinking often sets in. Most of us exercise choice effectively in some areas but not in others. Therefore, to avoid getting stuck in any area of your life, you need to:

Find your spots where you lose your freedom of choice.

These spots are different for everyone. Is it when someone refuses to give you what you need from them? Is it when someone gets angry? Is it when you hit an obstacle in the pursuit of a goal? Is it when your emotions are strong, or when you are depressed? When does it happen? How does it happen? Who is able to make it happen? When you learn the answers to those questions, you are on your way to freedom.

One woman who called into our radio program said that she was going to visit her family for Christmas, and she was getting depressed because she knew her grandfather would make things miserable, just as he always did. She dreaded hearing his criticism of her. We asked her why she had to listen to that, and she responded, "I just have to, that's all. I have no choice. That is what he does."

This woman lost her freedom the minute she walked in the door of that family gathering. She did not realize that no one can take away your freedom; she chose to give it up. As Paul tells us, "It is for freedom that Christ has set us free. Stand firm, then, and do not let yourselves be burdened again by a yoke of slavery" (Galatians 5:1 NIV). She was letting her grandfather "burden her with a yoke of slavery." He did not have the power to do that without her permission. But the family pressure to take it was so strong, that this was the place where she lost her choices.

As we talked, we quickly thought of several choices she could make:

- She could choose to not attend.

- She could choose to accept that he would be who he is, but she could give up the desire for his approval. That would empower her to ignore his remarks.

- She could empathize with him, "Gee, Grandfather, it seems like it's frustrating to you to have me be like I am. That sounds hard." She did not need to get hooked into convincing him of anything.

- She could steer clear of the grandfather at the gathering.

- She could call a friend throughout the gathering and give reports on how crazy he was, and they could laugh it off together.

- She could call him beforehand and ask if he planned to put her down this year as he had before. If he said yes, she could inform him that she might just go in another room when he started his put-downs. She wanted him to understand this beforehand, so he would not be surprised at her action.

The caller actually began to get lighthearted. Just the reminder that she did always have choices was a huge relief to her, as it is to all of us.

WE DON'T DO WELL IN PRISON BECAUSE WE WERE NOT DESIGNED FOR IT. We were designed to be free. And in some ways, life is a continual struggle to gain, regain, and live out our God-given freedom from the forces, both internal and external, that would take our freedom away.

Find out where your circle of freedom ends and take steps to enlarge it until you can feel free, no matter where you are, by remembering one thing: you always have choices! Ultimately, no person, or no circumstance has control of you—that control belongs to you and you only. So grasp God's hand and return to the freedom that he died to give you.

4

You Can Stretch and Risk

4

Only those who will risk going too far
can possibly find out how far one can go.
—T. S. ELIOT

When I (John) first started working in psychology, I was hired by a practice that provided me with an office, administrative support, client referrals, and collegial relationships. The working environment was helpful, with people I liked, and I gained a lot of good professional experience there. In time, however, I began wanting more autonomy, to do my own thing, and to hang out my own shingle. So I told the owner of the business what I was planning, and we worked out an arrangement that allowed me some time to transition from his practice to my new office, which I opened with a psychologist colleague.

It was exciting to sign the lease for my own office. I felt no fear at plunging into the new venture. After all, I was still working at the old place, and it was secure and well established. But my last day there was anything but exciting. I said goodbye to the staff at my going-away party, then I got in my car. I will never forget the thought that hit me as I drove to my new office: *What in the world was I thinking?*

I didn't have a full schedule of clients, and no one was providing new ones for me. The rent was due the first of the month, and I had signed a long-term lease. All the vision, energy, and optimism of my early stirrings to be on my own were replaced by fear and anxiety. I was truly on my own, and there was no safety net below me. I was really scared, and scared for a long period of time.

Fortunately, I did have several good friends who walked with me through this period. They listened, empathized, gave advice, and above all, they affirmed reality. They told me over and over that the plan I had originally conceived about going solo was still sound. They kept me grounded. And so I worked the plan: I spent a lot of time meeting other professionals and people helpers in my new community. I volunteered my services to organizations and churches. I spoke on psychological issues and relationships at various places in the area. I continued to receive training and supervision in my field.

And eventually the plan worked. In time the new office stabilized and became more established, and I could relax a little. The first of the month wasn't as terrifying as it had been earlier.

That was a long time ago. But here is the interesting part: Since those days, there have been many other work-related risks to take—everything from changing locations to new ventures and new jobs. Those risks have been real and genuine, with both downsides and upsides. I have been concerned, worried, and anxious, and I have prayed a lot. Still, *I have never been as scared or anxious as I was that first time.* It was different then, and I was different. I was facing the unknown with little experience at handling risk. So that first professional risk was a teacher for me. Better than any book or conversation with any expert, it took me through the experience of risk and showed me how to navigate, try things, make adjustments, and see the other side. Those first experiences have always served the purpose of helping me to face new risks with a little more confidence, courage, and faith.

Time to Get Out of the Boat!

Let's return to the purpose of this book: we want you to quit laying the blame for your failures on circumstance or other people. We want you to take charge of your dreams, goals, and obstacles, to maximize your chances for success. The way to do this is to start taking ownership of your life, and to activate the reality of those things that only you and no one else can do along your path. One of the keys to this life of ownership is *to become a person who is skilled at and unafraid of stretching and risking.* Perhaps you need to make a proposal to your boss about putting you in a better position. Maybe it's time to consider retraining or getting more education. It could be that you need to try new ways to conquer a bad habit. Or perhaps you need to have a serious confrontation with someone who is causing you problems. We all encounter situations similar to these, and often the only way to solve them is to stretch yourself and take risks. This chapter will help you understand the process and show you how to take the right steps.

To clarify what we're talking about, let's define stretching and risking as *actions toward a goal, which include a real possibility of danger.* This means moving into new territory with your eyes open, aware that you may suffer some loss or harm, but knowing that you have determined it to be worth the risk. To illustrate the downside risk in the examples above, your boss might be critical of your proposal. Your retraining may fail and cost you time and money. In spite of the effort you expend in trying to change that habit, it might even get worse. Your confrontation with the problem person might blow up in your face.

Not all risks are the same. There are smart risks and dumb risks. Smart risks are smart for two reasons: because your chances of success are reasonably good (the boss has been wanting you to take the initiative to make a proposal), or because the costs of failure are negligible (he doesn't like the proposal, but he still likes you and your work). Dumb risks are the converse: they have very low chances for success (the boss has never liked anyone's proposals in thirty years), or a high cost for failure (when people make proposals, he feels threatened and undermines their jobs). The important thing to remember here is that *you only need one of these two conditions to have a smart risk.*

In other words, a high probability of success will often trump a high cost for failure, so the high probability may be a green light to go for it. And a low cost for failure will often trump a low probability for success, so that may also be a green light. Too many people insist on both of the good assurances: I will probably succeed, and even if I don't, the downside is not a big deal. There is nothing wrong with that. Plunging ahead under these positive conditions is probably a good decision. But don't call it a risk. Along with those safe choices, you need a good sprinkling of smart risks to reach the goals and dreams you want.

People have been dealing with risk since the beginning of time; it's nothing new. God has always encouraged his people to take risks in order to grow, change, and live the lives of faith that will produce good fruit. No spiritual heroes have been able to avoid risks. They have all taken risks, and God has been with them. Remember the apostle Peter?

Then Peter called to him, "Lord, if it's really you, tell me to come to you by walking on water."

"All right, come," Jesus said.

So Peter went over the side of the boat and walked on the water toward Jesus. But when he looked around at the high waves, he was terrified and began to sink. "Save me, Lord!" he shouted.

Instantly Jesus reached out his hand and grabbed him. "You don't have much faith," Jesus said. "Why did you doubt me?" And when they climbed back into the boat, the wind stopped.

Then the disciples worshiped him. "You really are the Son of God!" they exclaimed. (Matthew 14:28–33 NLT)

You have to appreciate Peter's risky nature. Certainly he was impulsive. And he often failed miserably. But Peter was the one who always jumped out and tried something new. Where were the other guys? Significantly, Peter was also the man to whom, even with all his imperfections, Jesus gave the name, the Rock,[1] a title of stability, faith, and substance. Peter is the patron saint of *stretching and risking!* Peter learned maturity from his risks, and he ultimately succeeded in life.

Risks can do the same for you. So get out of the boat and see what happens!

Now we will walk you through the steps that show how to do this.

Make Change Your Ally

The first step is to get the big picture of the nature and value of *change*. For you to achieve your dreams and truly have a different life, work, and relationships, you need to see change as your friend, not your enemy. Change is tough, uncomfortable, and unsettling. But big successes always come from a willingness to change. People who learn to stretch themselves and risk have also learned to see the benefits and fruits of change, rather than to fear it and avoid it.

Simply put, change is about *things becoming different, as opposed to things remaining the same.* Change is dynamic; it means movement. It is not the status quo. We have no choice over some changes, such as growing older, occasional accidents, the economy, or another person's declining opinion about us. But, as we will see, we have choices over more than we think.

There are two types of change. Everyone wants one of them, but only those who are really ready for a better life want the other.

The first type is the *change of outcome.* An outcome is the end result you are looking for. A change of outcome refers to the fruit you want to reap; the differences you would like to see. Perhaps it is a slimmer you, a successful dating life, a passionate marriage, or a fulfilling career. Embracing a change of outcome is a good thing. It motivates, inspires, and keeps us focused on our goals.

But that is the easier part of change. It's easier because embracing the desire for a different outcome is a no-brainer. Like daydreaming, it puts positive images—a vision—in your mind. But merely embracing those images does not produce any benefits. It is necessary in order to develop vision, but it is not the hardest work.

The second, more potent, type of change is the *change of approach.* An approach is the way we go about achieving our outcomes and reaching our goals. A change of approach may be signing up with Weight Watchers, joining a dating service, insisting on having real talks about your marriage, or taking time off from work to figure out work. It means doing things differently, in a new way—a way that may be unfamiliar. But that's okay. For *when you don't change your approach, you are guaranteed to keep on getting what you are getting.* Or, as the quote attributed to Albert Einstein says, "Insanity is doing the same thing over and over again and expecting different results." That means when you resist changing what you are doing—even though it's not working—to get what you want, you are literally out of touch with reality. Crazy.

However, when you do change your approach, you receive, in turn, a change of outcome. The one is the key to the other. There is no free lunch here. We all would like life to be different and better; there's little fear or risk in wanting that. But the potential for a changed life is enormously greater for those who choose to change what they are doing.

Change can be work, and it can also be scary. You might have to admit you are wrong, that you have been going down the wrong path. Or you might have to bump up against someone's opposing opinion of the way things are. You might need to carve some time out to take a class. Or you might need to apologize to another person for not loving him or her with all your heart. More than anything, you will have to let go of the control you have, or attempt to have, over others. This book is about increasing your self-control—that is, control over your life. But *you can't really have self-control until you give up other-control.*

We are all control freaks, to an extent. We would like for our lives, our relationships, and our jobs to operate as we would like them to operate. I have had more than one business friend with a work problem state something like this: "If my organization would just do it my way, we'd be okay." Perhaps. But usually the real truth was that these friends didn't have all the correct data either to justify their way or to criticize the organization's way. They were simply more comfortable trying to control others' responses to bring them in line with their own rather than face the possibility that their own outlook should change.

A friend of mine is the mother of a teenage son who has attention deficit hyperactivity disorder, or ADHD. It's a clear diagnosis—not the kind that doctors sometimes make to cover a lack of structure and discipline in the home. The family has a lot of healthy love and structure, and the boy is a responsible person. He genuinely has the condition, and he is on medication to help him focus and think better. However, he didn't like the hassle of taking the medicine or the feeling of being less than normal that came with needing it. So, as is common in teens, he wanted to stop. My friend came to me and said, "How can I make him take the medication? He needs it."

"What have you tried so far?" I asked.

"I've reminded him that he needs it and tried to get him to take it," she replied. "I've even thought about putting him on restriction until he takes it."

I thought for a minute and then said, "Let him not take it for a few days."

"Are you nuts?" she said. "He won't be able to pay attention in class, study, or do homework."

"Maybe," I said. "But try it anyway."

She didn't like the idea, but she wasn't getting anywhere with her own methods, so she agreed.

A few days later, I asked how things were. "It's funny," she answered. "He loved being free of the pills the first couple of days. But on the third day, he was asked to leave a couple of classes because he was clowning around. Then he forgot his homework, and he bombed a test in a class where he'd been making straight A's."

"What happened then?" I asked.

"Well, I didn't say anything, though I really wanted to. But before he went to bed that night, he said to me, 'Mom, I think I need my pills. Just don't be triumphant about it!'"

We both laughed at his comment, but the lesson was serious. My friend made an important change that caused great fruit in her son's life. She stopped reminding and nagging him and let him experience life without the medications. The best part of this is that *the boy is now the one who is owning and taking responsibility for his own care, not his mom.* He is on his way to becoming a grownup.

I was pretty sure that the outcome would be good, because I knew this boy; he really cares about doing well in high school and wants to get into a good college. Had that not been the case, I might have given different advice. Was this mom's change uncomfortable and difficult? It was indeed. And yet, because she was willing to take the risk, try something different, and give up control of the situation, they are both much better off.

Get Rid of Inertia

In the world of physics, inertia is the tendency for things to stay the way they are. If you throw a baseball, it will go in the same direction unless some external force, like a bat, changes its direction. Another law of inertia that applies to change is this: it takes more energy to get a stationary object moving than it does to change the direction of an object in motion. You have to work harder to get a ball in the air than to change the direction of a moving ball.

These principles of inertia also apply to your personal life and to your drive for success. We all have a tendency to resist change and to keep things just as they are. That is inertia. But it's more difficult to change if you're going nowhere than to change if you're headed somewhere, *even if you are going in the wrong direction.* When you are already moving, it's easier to correct your course.

For example, I have a friend who was in his mid-thirties before he found his career. He made a lot of wrong moves and took a lot of jobs that weren't a fit for him. But he kept looking, asking, searching, and exploring. He had financial setbacks, though he never let his family go into jeopardy. He never settled into "I guess this is the best I can do, but I don't enjoy it." He never blamed anyone. He just kept swinging the bat, going to meetings, asking questions, and doing research. Finally, he got involved in the media industry, which was a perfect fit for him. He has now been happy in that field for many years.

Be like my friend. Get rid of inertia; decide now to start making some changes. A bad decision is better than no decision, as the Marine Corps says. Become a moving object. As long as you're moving, it will take God less energy to change your direction!

Enjoy the Ride

It's not enough to just grit your teeth and say, "Okay, I'll start being open to change." Such a response is half-hearted and fear-based, and you will end up sabotaging yourself. Instead, you need to learn to experience change as positive, beneficial, and often enjoyable. The ride can be fun, sometimes even exhilarating.

I often hear people who resist change use negative, inertia-based statements such as, "That will never work," or "That's a crazy idea," or "I guess things are okay like they are." Such responses reflect their feeling that changes are bad and painful. On the other hand, I hear people who like change saying such things as, "That idea might just be weird enough to work," or "What's a way to look at this that no one has ever seen?," or "We're in a rut and it's boring; let's shake things up."

I like being around this second group. They are open, expectant, and don't fear the unknown. Become a member of that group.

Face and Reject Your Fears

When I am consulting with businesspeople about their organization or counseling people about their relationships, I usually experience a predictable progression of events. First, we go over the goal or problem situation. Then we look at what efforts they have already made that haven't been effective. Then we get into the deeper issues of what is underneath the conflict or problem. After that, we look at new solutions. Now, what happens next is generally some sort of resistance, excuse, or evasion: the clients usually give me reasons the solutions won't work. But I expect that to happen, and so we continue.

Next we often get to another layer below the resistance which explains the resistance: a layer of fear. When people can admit to themselves, *I am afraid of stretching and risking in this relationship, or in this job, or dealing with my habits,* we are getting extremely close to success.

That may sound counterintuitive, but it is true. How can admitting a negative thing like fear get you closer to a great life? The answer is that when you can understand your fears of risk, you are free to reject them. And this freedom leads to another: the freedom to take new steps to new paths of success. When you don't know your fears, you can't deal with them. They remain in charge of your life, and you are powerless.

Helpful and Useless Fear

Just as there are smart and dumb risks, there are also helpful and useless fears. Like any emotion, fear serves as a signal to us. It alerts us to a potentially dangerous situation and prepares us to take protective action. That is why there is a physiological component to fear: increased heart rate, adrenal surges, and muscle tension. These responses prepare us for flight from harm. So fear is helpful when there is a truly dangerous situation ahead of us, and when we need to take evasive action. If your company is going bankrupt, your fear of financial problems may be helping you to get your resume out and get moving on the next job. That helpful fear is grounded in reality.

At the same time, some fears are useless to us and keep us from the risks we need to take. These useless fears are not about reality, but more about misperceptions and distortions we have in our heads. We need to learn to pay attention to the one, and get rid of the other.

For example, I love rock music, and used to play in a band when I was a student. When I grew up and started working, I figured that my playing days were over, and I resigned myself to being a listener, not a performer. One day, however, I was talking to some neighbors, and they mentioned an upcoming rehearsal. My ears pricked up and I asked them what they were rehearsing for. They told me they were in a rock band. I was surprised that these businessmen, who were also husbands and fathers, were playing in a rock band. I now know that this is far more common than I had realized back then.

Anyway, I told them I also liked playing and asked if they needed another person. If so, could I audition. They said sure, and they told me when and where to be.

Immediately after I made the commitment, I experienced fear and anxiety. It was nothing crippling, but it was enough to make me consider coming up with some excuse and canceling the audition. I felt both helpful and useless fears. I list some of them here, along with my counter thought.

- *What if I'm not good enough for the band, and these guys think poorly of me?* Useless. The guys aren't that way, and anyway, if I'm not good enough, maybe I can get lessons and improve.

- *What if I'm no good and they let me in because they are nice guys and they feel sorry for me?* Useless. They aren't going to ruin the band to be nice. And besides, we would all know in a few months whether it's working or not.

- *What if I get in a band and my other friends and family tell me I'm attempting to re-enter my adolescence?* Useless. If they say that, I'll get feedback and see if there's some psychological reason I shouldn't be doing this. But until then, there's no reason not to audition.

- *What if it takes too much time from my family?* Helpful. Any personal interest has to be measured in terms of relationships, values, and obligations.

- *What if the equipment costs a lot of money?* Helpful. Time to talk to my wife about how much room we have in the hobby budget.

As it turned out, the audition went well, and for several years the hobby has been a lot of fun. But the point here is for you to learn which fears are helpful—that is, grounded in reality—and which are useless—because they are based on your own misperceptions. When you deal with your useless fears, you are much more able to choose freely and well which risks you should take.

Your Fear List

Fears, like bad dreams, are best disposed of in the light of day. Expose your fears to yourself and others you trust. Identify them and where they came from. They are much less powerful when you can look at them in the light. Say to yourself, *I have not taken a risk in an important area of my life because I am afraid that:*

- *I will lose a relationship.* Are you sure? Or will that person just get mad and withdraw for a while?

- *Someone will get mad at me.* The anger of others is unpleasant, but you must be able to tolerate people being mad at you to be successful.[2]

- *I might hurt somebody's feelings.* Certainly, you could. But hurt and harm are two different things. You don't want to harm, but discomfort can be a help to someone.

- *I might lose my job.* Check out the reality of that fear with someone who is balanced. Is the situation truly that fragile?

- *I might fail.* You might. You might not. And failure is often a blessing.

- *I might be disappointed.* That is possible. And when you are, call a friend, get a pep talk, and get back up again.

- *I will be out of control.* If you have strong feelings that emerge, deal with them with someone who can help you express and understand them.

- *I won't know what will happen next.* Right, but you have a pretty good idea. Don't wait until there is a 100 percent guarantee of the outcome.

- *I might have feelings I don't want to have.* Yes, feelings can be uncomfortable, but they don't last forever.

- *I will be worse off than if I had never taken the chance.* Certainly you shouldn't risk everything on a long shot. But will you later regret missing the window of opportunity you have now to make the situation better?

I hope you don't think I am trivializing your fears; I am not. Fears are real, and they are quite painful. But always submit your fears to reality. See if it's your past talking, or a critical person you've given too much power to, or if things truly are as bad as you fear. It is a helpful exercise.

Learn How to Address Fear and Reject It

Working through the list above won't abolish all fear for all time. Life is not like that. Even though you can become a person who faces change and takes risks, you will always be faced with anxiety, concern, and scared feelings when the unknown danger appears. But you can reject fear when you understand it, and when you understand where it gets its power to paralyze you.

Fear of Fear

As any psychologist will tell you, fear is stronger when we fear becoming afraid. This is called the fear of fear. Suppose you need to confront the boss about his attitude, but you are afraid that he might retaliate. So you stay happy and positive on the outside but remain dissatisfied on the inside.

The longer you ignore the fear, the more you will activate it. And since the fear is associated with an uncomfortable outcome, having it burrow around in your mind naturally gives you an uncomfortable feeling. Eventually you learn to avoid thinking about the fearful situation so you won't have to keep feeling the fear. And the more you avoid feeling that fear, the more afraid of it you become. It is a vicious cycle, and it doesn't help you reach your dreams.

If you are experiencing this downward spiral, begin allowing yourself to tolerate fear. Let yourself feel the anxiety and scared feelings you have about your boss's wrath. The more you do this, the more you will realize that things might get unpleasant, but you can make it through his anger. Now you can allow the fear to enter your mind, acknowledge it for what it is, and let it go. Facing fear helps you to no longer fear your fear. The power is greatly reduced.

Self-Control and Power

Another aspect of fear is that *the less control and power you feel, the greater the fear.* Fear is a danger signal. It says, "Protect yourself! Run!" And if you don't feel any sense of control or power over your life and choices, you experience yourself as powerless, unsafe, and vulnerable. You are at the mercy of the danger, and you can't protect yourself. It is a horrible feeling, and it gives fear a strength it shouldn't have.

The antidote is to see the reality that you are not helpless. You have choices, all the choices that a mature adult has. You're not your boss's slave, victim or little child. You can relate to him, talk to him as an adult, and, if you have to, protect yourself from any toxicity he might throw at you. Remind yourself that you have choices. This will give you access to all the control and power you need.

Support and Reality Checks

It always helps to have a few friends you can confess your fears to—friends who can weigh them from their more uninvolved viewpoint. Tell them what you're afraid of and say, "I need a reality check here. Am I listening to a fear that is real or just in my head?" They can help provide insight, perspective, and encouragement for you to push through the fear.

I once had to confront a certain person about a problem, and I was really afraid of his reaction. He was defensive and blamey, and I had seen him tear into people who told him the truth. But I needed to do it for his family and him. I had a couple of friends call me on my cell phone a few hours before my meeting just to say, "This is a reality check. You're doing the right thing, and I'm in your corner." It meant a great deal to me, and I was able to go through with the conversation. It was bad, and he blasted away at me, but I was able to listen, stay neutral, and still be direct about the problem. And because I did, and because it happened in the right way, he and his family were eventually a lot better off.

TRY THINGS THAT ARE BEYOND YOU

My first job out of college was as a houseparent in a children's home. Here I was, a twenty-three-year-old recent graduate, living in a cottage with seven teenage boys. I didn't know then how much I didn't know, and I am glad now that I didn't.

One of the kids on campus, a large and muscular sixteen-year-old named Paul, absolutely hated me. He was from another cottage, and I had caught him sneaking out one night. In his mind, I had no authority to report him because he wasn't one of my kids. So when I did, he went on a mission to make me miserable. Paul would walk into a room where I was, with other people present, and cuss me out. He would threaten me when others couldn't hear. To my dismay, he had a reputation for being a good fighter, so there was substance behind his threats. Also, he would urge other kids to disobey me. In time, his mission worked. Though the other workers and I tried all the right things—talking with Paul, working on the relationship, setting limits, and warning him of more limits, his bad behavior was escalating and getting more out of control. He didn't care about the consequences; he wanted to hurt me.

I had no idea what to do. Things were going from bad to worse. Then one day, Ray, my boss, who was truly gifted with kids, said to me, "Have a boxing match with Paul."

"*What!?*" I said.

"I think you need to box with Paul."

"You have got to be kidding!"

"Well, hear me out," Ray said. "Nothing is working, right? And I think sometimes a really angry kid like Paul needs to experience his aggression with your own aggression, in real life. He has this vendetta thing, and I think his mind is getting more and more angry and powerful, because there's nowhere for him to go with the anger. He never had a dad he could face in order to experience healthy conflict. And so his anger has a life of its own. Also, I think it will be kind of a connection between you and him. Sort of like the bond that opposing athletes feel for each other after a game."

I said, "No. You're nuts. No."

Ray said, "Well, it's just an idea. But think about it, okay?"

I did think about it. Meanwhile, during the next couple of days, Paul got more and more crazy, and we were beginning to consider shipping him to a more structured environment. Finally I thought, *What the heck.*

So the match was scheduled. Three rounds. The children's home went mad with anticipation. It was every kid's dream to have one of their own annihilate an authority figure. As for me, I didn't know anything about boxing, so a friend of mine hurriedly gave me some lessons.

On the day of the match, I was sick to my stomach. I walked into the room where a makeshift ring had been assembled. Sixty kids were surrounding it, yelling for Paul to kill me. When the bell rang, we went after each other. Paul was much quicker and more experienced in boxing than I was, but I had a little size edge on him, and maybe I could strategize a little better. Anyway, I survived the three rounds, and most people called it a draw. (Actually, I think Paul won.)

Ray was dead on. Paul changed toward me. We never became close, but the harassment ended. He would say hello when we saw each other, and when I asked him how things were going, he always had a little something to say. Some sort of positive connection had been forged between us, as well as a little mutual respect. I left the home later that year, and I never saw Paul again. But I still think about him from time to time and wish him well.

I don't recommend Ray's solution to others. I think it was his intuitive genius that inspired him in those unique circumstances, never to be repeated. And I was way out of my comfort zone, literally. But the combination of factors—the reality that nothing was working, along with my respect for Ray, as well as my own early twenties' impulsivity—created a way to try something that was very much beyond me. It wasn't beyond me physically, perhaps, but certainly beyond any idea I had that I was capable of doing something as foolhardy as boxing a fighter kid. And good things resulted.

The Stretch

This is what stretching yourself is all about. Successful people are always extending themselves, trying new things, and getting out of their comfort zones. That is the way life works and how we were designed. There is no stagnant position in growth and life. We are either moving forward or moving backward. And here is the reality that requires the stretch: *that which you desire will require more of you than you are today.*

What do you dream of and desire? I hope your dreams are big ones; dreaming big is the only way to grow through life. But at the same time, big dreams will demand big things of you. You may find that you need to try things you can't do now. That means you will need to develop abilities and capacities that will reach the dream.

For example, I have a good friend who has always dreamed of becoming a psychologist. She is very drawn to the process of connecting deeply with people's emotions and understanding the core of their being in order to help them grow and heal. She is a single mom, so her education track doesn't fit the typical model of going straight to grad school after you get your bachelor's degree. But that has not been her biggest obstacle. The thing that was really beyond her was the math and statistics requirements of grad school. In her previous life, she majored in fine arts, and she always hated and avoided math. Now she has this goal that includes coursework and a required exam in math and stats. It was a big deal.

However, she wasn't going to let it stop her. So she signed up for courses, hired tutors, and took practice exams in these subjects she had shunned. It was really painful at first, as she had never worked her brain in these areas—never mind the fact that she hadn't been in school for many years. But in time, *what was beyond her became a part of her.* Now she can hardly believe that she actually understands math and statistics at a quite sophisticated level. It never would have happened had she not been willing to stretch herself.

Look at your own situation. Does your dream require more of you than you presently have? To become more confrontive and assertive in your relationships? To learn a new skill, such as accounting, computers, or sales techniques? To know your way around the Bible and grasp theological concepts? To master listening skills for a certain position? *Just because you can't do these things today doesn't mean you won't be able to do them tomorrow.* The upcoming discussion on persistence (see chapter 8) will go into detail on how to engage the stretching process that will get you there.

When you reach the end of your abilities is when you truly live. We were designed to change, try new things, fail, learn, and become better people. Those individuals who have stopped reaching beyond themselves have stopped living. The research on aging supports this idea. As people get older, those who continue learning things—from dancing to rock climbing to real estate—stay healthier and more alert. The mind's ability to change is technically known as plasticity, and it means that our minds adapt and grow as we require them to. But if we don't require anything of our minds, they begin to deteriorate. It's the "use it or lose it" principle.

Not only that, but when you learn new life skills to achieve your goal or solve your problem, you receive another benefit. *Those skills will have value in achieving other goals as well.* Life skills that were previously beyond you can often be applied to many areas of life and give you more success, competence, and mastery over your other plans and dreams. Becoming more equipped for business, or personal growth, or learning about addictions, or parenting, can affect so many other parts of your world. For example, my friend who now knows math is also more competent in her personal finances. And my own experience with Paul helped me to learn how to deal effectively with someone who hated me. (I assure you, however, that I have found other ways besides boxing!)

Think, Then Do

Those people who are adept at stretching and risking have the skill of *thinking and doing.* This may sound overly simple, but many people don't have this skill. As a result, they often end up not living the lives they would love to live. Let me explain. Any goal that requires risk, whether it's investing your effort, having an important conversation, or trying to break into a new industry, will also require a process to best engage in that risk. Basically, this means that smart risk takers think through the matter thoroughly, then, if it seems worth the risk, they do it. They take the plunge and jump into the water. They have learned when it's time to think and analyze, and when it's time to stop and get on with it. That's the process—thinking and doing. In successful scenarios, the one goes before the other.

When my father and mother were dating in our home state of North Carolina, she got a call to audition for a large opera company in New York City. She was a highly talented coloratura soprano, and there was a great deal of interest in her. In fact, she got an offer to move there and join the company.

This offer gave my dad a couple of hard things to deal with. He really valued her musical giftedness and wanted her to be a success. Yet her move to New York would present difficulties for the relationship. On the other hand, marriages had survived that sort of distance. He thought long and hard about the situation, evaluating both sides of the issue. But finally, he reached a decision and told Mom, "If you go, we're over."

She really did not want to hear that. Singing in the opera was her lifelong dream. Yet she was very much in love with Dad and wanted a life with him. She was placed in a position where, either way, she would lose something quite important to her. She weighed the alternatives and eventually decided not to go to New York. Now, with well over fifty years of marriage behind them, she agrees that Dad made the right move with her. It cost her a lot, but she has no regrets.

At the time, Dad didn't know whether it would turn out to be the right move or not. He didn't have a lot of time to figure it out. She would leave by a certain date, and he had to decide whether to act or to let things just follow the course they were on. If he forced her to make a choice, he risked losing her forever. If he did nothing, however, he risked losing her to long distance. To do nothing was to choose something. So he deliberated as much as he could, and then he took the gamble. He decided to act.

There is a time to think, deliberate, analyze, and pray. Then there is a time to act.

When you are considering a big risk, do your thinking well. Get all the information, perspective, and wisdom you can. Understand the nature of the benefits and the cost. Jesus taught this principle in a metaphor about building: "Suppose one of you wants to build a tower. Will he not first sit down and estimate the cost to see if he has enough money to complete it?" (Luke 14:28 NIV). This is a necessary step. Successful people may risk, but they don't equate risk with impulsivity.

At the same time, however, the thinking step must end and give way to the risk. My dad only had so much time or he would have missed his opportunity. We have a tendency to want all of the answers before jumping into the water: Will it hold me up? Is it too cold? How deep is it? When Peter decided to leave the boat and meet Jesus on the water, he didn't have a focus group to tell him how to walk out. We have a term for the demand to have all the information before one acts: we call it the paralysis of analysis. People often obsess and worry, trying to manage the risk to the point that the open door will close. That is not how stretching, risking, or faith works. At some point, you must use your best judgment and make a choice. Make it. That's all anyone can do.

Finally, when you risk, do it all the way. If you can't take the risk wholeheartedly, it might be better to pass on it rather than be halfway about it. If you can't truly plunge into the risk and follow through with it, then you will experience the pain of the risk but never its benefits. Taking risk halfway trains you to believe that this process doesn't work. Better far to make the leap knowing that you'll either get what you want, or that you did your best and can learn from your failure.

Last year, I went on a whitewater rafting trip with my sons, along with another father and his son. During a break from the river, we hiked up to a canyon where we found a natural pool of water. A high rock formation extended over the edge of the pool, creating a natural diving platform. Everyone took turns making the jump, except for my friend's son who had no experience jumping off heights. He was a great athlete, but he'd never had a chance to try anything like this. Still, he climbed to the top of the formation. He walked to the edge and looked down. He edged back a couple of feet, then walked forward again. Then he did it again. And again. By this time the rest of us knew he was struggling. We yelled encouragement, and we also yelled that it was okay not to jump. We really wanted to support him. Back to the edge, and then back to safety he went, over and over. I could not tell how this would play out, and I really felt bad for him and his predicament. He was trying to be brave, but his fear was strong. But finally he screwed up his courage, took the leap, and landed in the water. We all applauded and cheered his success, for we knew what taking that plunge meant to him.

When you are ready to stop thinking and start taking the risk, there can be no going back. You can't reverse your direction in midair. Think where you are now. What risk lies ahead for you that will help you achieve your dream? Will you need to give up free nights to get training? Or walk up to the person you are dating and say that you can't see him anymore if he doesn't change a bad behavior? Or quit a job and go on a search for the right one? Or admit to someone that you have an addiction that you are afraid might be gaining control of your life?

The good news is that midair is one of those places where God loves to meet us. He knows how scary risk is. And he knows that what we need most in those times when we are suspended above the ground is the knowledge of his presence, his support, and his grace:

> Do not fear, for I am with you;
> Do not anxiously look about you, for I am your God.
> I will strengthen you, surely I will help you,
> Surely I will uphold you with My righteous right hand.
> (Isaiah 41:10 NASB)

Blessed are you when you stretch and risk to find your dreams. He is on your side.

5

You Can Get Connected

5

Talent wins games, but teamwork and intelligence win championships.
—MICHAEL JORDAN

Kevin, a friend of mine (John), is enormously successful in the construction industry. He is at the top of his field, well respected, and earns a great deal of money. At the same time, he is a person of great spiritual depth and commitment who gives generously to many causes.

From time to time, however, Kevin takes heat from people in his industry who don't know him personally. A few people, mainly competitors, sometimes tell others that he is not a team player and does things too much on his own. I asked him about this one day.

"Do you attribute your success to being the loner," I asked, "picking yourself up by your bootstraps, and all that?"

He thought for a moment. "Most of the time, I find that the perception that I'm a loner comes from people who don't know me well. I can certainly be hardheaded, and I am pretty opinionated about my work, to a fault. Maybe that's where the reputation comes from. But whatever success I have does not come from being a loner; it comes from the opposite."

"What do you mean?"

"Well, I have constructed my life around being with people in all sorts of ways that help me succeed. I am in a personal spiritual-growth group, where I am accepted, supported, and pushed to be a better person. I have a few professional colleagues from whom I get industry perspective. I have a great administrative and support team that fills in all the gaps in my own abilities. They are behind the scenes, but they make me look good. I have a mentor who guides me in the big picture issues of my direction and path. My wife is my confidante, and she has made more suggestions than I can count, which have helped my professional growth immensely."

Kevin ended with a rhetorical question: "So I guess that's how lone rangers operate?"

Kevin gives us a key to how every truly successful person functions and thrives. They do not do it in a vacuum. They do not pick themselves up by their bootstraps. Although they are highly independent and do have their own values and opinions, they are still closely connected to the outside world, where one finds the resources for success.

If you choose to be a loner or insist on being independent of others, remaining in isolation and self-sufficiency, your failure to achieve your dreams and goals can be charged to no one but you. It will be your own fault.

THE ECOSYSTEM OF SUCCESS

If you want to get ahead of the pack and achieve relational and career success, you need to understand that success operates much like an ecosystem.

Ecosystem is a term from biology that describes a community of interacting organisms and their environment. A simple example of an ecosystem is a jungle. In the jungle, the sun provides energy to sustain plants, which feed herbivorous animals, which in turn feed carnivorous animals, and all the animals help fertilize the plants. Each component interacts with the other components in some way. The jungle is not a single thing; it is a system, and it only works successfully because it is a system.

Successful people understand that we are designed to function in a similar way. We operate at our peak levels when we work and network within our own ecosystem. God has created resources within our environment that we must interact with and receive from, or we will ultimately fail. Those who achieve their hearts' desires rely on their ecosystems and get connected to the resources they need.

The self-made man (or woman) is actually an absurdity. He may think he is self-made, but if you look below the surface you will always find that he owes a great deal of credit to other resources in his life that he may not be aware of.

Some people resist the idea that they are dependent on connections with others. They don't want to appear weak, needy, or incomplete. They equate dependence on others with childishness, and it clashes with their view of what an adult should be. Or they may be concerned that connectedness puts them at the mercy of unscrupulous people who might set them back. Some people are simply too prideful to stoop to dependence. Or some idealize the fictional heroes of our culture such as Tom Cruise's *Mission: Impossible* and Bruce Willis's *Die Hard* characters.

Our need for connectedness is, at heart, a spiritual issue and a spiritual reality. God designed us to do better in life when we are connected to the right people and the right things. We simply don't get ahead when we are disconnected from those people and those things. When you look at the grand design of Creation, you see that from the start God meant us to interact, reach out, and be connected in all sorts of ways. Here are his first instructions to Adam and Eve in the beginning of time:

> God blessed them and told them, "Multiply and fill the earth and subdue it. Be masters over the fish and birds and all the animals." And God said, "Look! I have given you the seed-bearing plants throughout the earth and all the fruit trees for your food. And I have given all the grasses and other green plants to the animals and birds for their food." And so it was. Then God looked over all he had made, and he saw that it was excellent in every way. (Genesis 1:28–31 NLT)

The first human couple had God, one another, and a world of resources that they were in charge of. That world was given for their own benefit and nourishment, and in turn, they were charged to take good care of it. It was never the plan for us to reach deep inside ourselves, find the strength we need, and willpower our way to happiness and success. The sources of life have always been outside us, not inside.

Recently I had a far-reaching business decision to make. It involved my sense of my own mission in life, my focus, my direction, and what it would take to get me where I wanted to go. It was also a highly complex matter, and whichever choice I made would change things for me in a pretty radical way. So I really wanted to take the right path. To go the wrong direction would be costly—professionally, financially, and personally.

I thought long and hard. Actually, in my heart, I really wanted God to make this decision for me. I was looking for a sign, a miracle, a voice in the night, a burning bush—it didn't matter as long as it was clearly a signal from God. The reality was that I didn't want to take ownership of the consequences of my decision. I didn't like the idea of the wrong choice being my fault. I wanted to blame God, not myself, if anything went wrong. I wanted him to do both his job and mine in determining my direction.

One day during this period I was reading my Bible and asking him to show me what to do. "I'll do whatever you say," I said, "just make it clear to me." And I was really sincere. The scripture passage in my devotional plan for that day was in the book of wisdom, Proverbs. I thought, *A wisdom passage. This is cool. I'll read the wise solution here and get moving.* So I read, "Leave your simple ways behind, and begin to live; learn to use good judgment" (Proverbs 9:6 NLT).

I couldn't believe it. I reread the passage. It said the same thing. I really didn't like what I was seeing. I didn't think God would just kick the decision back to me and hang me out to dry. Still, the passage seemed to be saying something like that, and it certainly wasn't what I wanted to hear. But as I thought on it more, I began to realize what I was reading.

I was to leave my simple ways behind: I had been thinking in a very simplistic manner that God would tell me what to do directly. And he does that sometimes. But not all the time. This time, I was not to demand that the answer come to me the easy way—directly from God. *I was to begin to live:* In the Bible life always involves connectedness to relationship. When we are disconnected from God and others, we are separated from life and from what is most important. I was truly connecting to him, but I wasn't connecting to people, which is a big part of the spiritual life. *I was to learn to use good judgment:* I didn't want to do any evaluation or analysis of the matter. It was too complicated and overwhelming, with too many variables. I just wanted words of fire written on the wall telling me exactly what to do.

As far as I could tell, the message for me was this: I was to quit asking for God to make my decision for me, and instead use the resources he had already put in my environment to discover the answer. So that day I spent an hour or two thinking, analyzing, and calling a couple of my close friends, who spent a lot of time unpacking the complexities of the issue with me. Soon a pattern and a path began emerging from all the chaos in my mind. Using all I had gleaned from praying, getting advice, and using my best judgment, I closed in on what, as far as I could tell, was the right way to go. All the sources seemed to correspond with each other, and they felt consistent to me. So I chose my path, and it ended up being the right decision.

The real breakthroughs happened when I went over the issues with my friends and interacted with their perspectives. Things started moving when I entered the ecosystem.

All this is to say that success comes when we submit to the way God designed things and take advantage of the ecosystem we're in. When we do that, we are moving with the river current of reality, not paddling desperately against it. What I learned is this: *you will succeed in your dreams to the extent that you connect to the external world.* Connection is that critical.

FIND THE FUEL

Connections are the gasoline providing the drive and energy you need to reach your destination, whether it is solving a relational problem, finding your dream career, building a healthy marriage, or conquering a troublesome habit. You need to know where the fuel is, and how to get it into your tank.

Successful people turn not just to a single source, but to several to find the connectedness they need. Your journey will be filled with many different challenges, and one source of connection will not be adequate to meet all of them. Each connection will supply one of the fuels you need for that particular facet of the journey. In the next several pages we will introduce and discuss some of the primary sources for the fuels you will require.

Fuel Source No. 1: God

Though it seems to go without saying, God is the connection we need most to find success. It's important to not think about this need as some religious abstraction, as when people say, "Religion is a good thing for people; it gives them peace and helps them solve their problems." The truth is much bigger than that. It is good for us to trust and believe in God, not because it helps decrease our blood pressure or calms us down or improves our mental health. Exercise and journaling could do that!

Connecting to God is making an attachment in a very real, profound, yet also a practical way, with reality itself. He is the Author of reality. As Creator and Designer of the way life should work, he empowers, guides, and supports our efforts to have a better life and better relationships. God is in both the background and the foreground of these matters.

Therefore, it is much more than merely a good and practical move to reach out to God for help with our success journey. It is a necessary and critical move. Success doesn't happen outside of him. We need him and his help, and it is impossible to find our way out of bad situations and into better ones without his leading and his hand.

In ancient times when Israel was a kingdom, its leaders stayed connected and dependent on God for their success and dreams, and for those of the nation. Over time, however, these leaders began to disconnect, to go their own way and lean on themselves. Though God continually invited them to return to dependence on him, they listened to false prophets and, more often than not, walked away from the connection. As a result, over time the kingdom deteriorated and was finally destroyed. Israel's people were dispossessed from their own land for many years. During the kingdom's last days, as the nation was being attacked by invaders, one of its true prophets named Isaiah spoke God's words to the people.

During the twilight of the nation, the leaders in the capital city of Jerusalem were trying to defend and fortify themselves against imminent enemy aggression. They wanted to make sure they had enough water to withstand a siege. Anyone would call this an important task to resolve problems and achieve success! But God's response was not encouraging: "Between the city walls, you build a reservoir for water from the old pool. But all your feverish plans are to no avail because you never ask God for help. He is the one who planned this long ago" (Isaiah 22:11 NLT).

Those words were addressed to Israel, but the truth behind them is timeless and still of great value for us in today's context. Don't let this passage draw you into the question of which matters: God's will or our efforts. The relevant point for your success is that it certainly makes sense to work hard at making your plans, but it makes just as much sense to ask God for help. His nature is to help and guide his people. He is the foundation of any dreams you want to achieve.

Check in with God about all aspects of your efforts to have a better life. Tell him you have a desire, a dream, and a passion to build a company, or find a relationship, or start a ministry to people who need it, or heal a broken relationship. Submit that desire to him; ask if it is from him and if it fits his plan for you. His affirmation is one aspect of the connection. But there is more. Go further and ask him not only to affirm your dream, but also to give you the strength, the guidance, and the wisdom to make it all happen. Ask him to open doors, to change people's minds, and to give you opportunities and ideas you have never had before. He is invested in our success if it originates from him and advances his kingdom and his values. When you are connected to him in your dream, you can "delight yourself in the LORD; and He will give you the desires of your heart" (Psalm 37:4 NASB). The desire you feel within you has its birth within him.

God is the source of all your connection fuel. But, as in my own example above, he connects with us both directly and indirectly. We look not only to him, but also to the connections he places in our environment—our ecosystem. Let's look at some of the indirect types of connection fuel God sends that can propel you toward your goals.

Fuel Source No. 2: Relationships That Guard Your Life

People who are escaping a culture of blame and entering the world of success create a team around themselves. They understand that we all need a few people surrounding us who are in our corner. This team is composed of individuals who are with you and for you. They are willing to be involved in your life, to help guard and protect it. They have the time and commitment to walk with you each step of the way. They are the ones you turn to when you feel crazy, discouraged, or like a total screw-up. In a sense they are family, the relational "home" you go to for help, support, and encouragement. As the saying goes when friends support one another: "I've got your back."

These connections serve a particular purpose. They are not people you go to for specific, technical competency or specialized information. They provide a foundation of safety, validation, feedback, confrontation, and cheerleading. Information-based connections are also important, for they primarily guard your dream. We will show you what those are about in the next section.

You don't need many people on your relationship team; in fact a large number doesn't really work. It takes a lot of time to develop a relationship in which the people know each other well and there is deep trust. Quality is much more important than quantity. When choosing your team, don't make easy availability the primary requirement. My experience is that people who have all the time in the world are often not much in demand for a reason. People who have something to offer you are probably offering it to someone else as well, and you may have to carve out time for your relationship with them.

If you want to realize your dreams, you will likely need to put some structure on these relationships. For example, I have been in a personal growth and support group for many years. The relationships in that group began as casual friendships that involved occasional lunches and evenings out. Gradually, however, we all noticed a *simpatico* of values, directions, and personality styles. We have widely different personality styles, but that keeps it interesting. All this was happening before the small-group phenomenon emerged in the church world, so I wasn't thinking along those lines at all. But I began to notice that I found myself going to these individuals for support and advice more and more. When I had a dream or a problem, I would call them first. When I wanted to do something socially, they were on my mind. And the same was true with them. We all sought each other out for encouragement, support, and social involvement. At some point we all began to realize that it might help to meet on some sort of regular basis. We became aware that we needed continuity and structure in our social relationships, so we decided to form a group and start meeting together for life support, prayer, and personal growth.

Now I cannot imagine going through life without these people. We have been through just about everything together, including parenting stuff, marriage issues, life stresses, career questions, personal failures and struggles, and spiritual quests. We know each other extremely well, and there are few if any secrets among us. When work or travel causes me to miss our meetings, I find myself wishing I had their support and input. Life is better with these folks, and it's not the same without them.

In terms of dreams and success, this group has been crucial for all its members. We know one another's goals and passions, and we keep ourselves up to speed on them. We also make sure that we connect outside of the goals. It's important to connect with the heart and soul beneath the dream, and not just with the dream itself. That is what you need your team to do. They need to know the life you lead, your background, your character, and your weaknesses. Otherwise, they cannot really fuel your progress toward your goals.

This is an important point. You need to bring all of yourself to your team, not just your idea of where you want to go. Focusing on your goals without attending to yourself is like attempting to make your e-mail software work better when your operating system is broken. With computers, the operating system always trumps the application.

Everything stops until the OS is working, because it is the architecture undergirding everything else. You don't want to handicap your team's support for you by neglecting to be vulnerable, open, and honest about who you really are and what you really need.

So build your team, and choose its members well. Find people who care about you. Who have similar values. Who are relational, nonjudgmental, but still direct and honest with you. And who are available on a regular basis. The ideal is to find those who want the same support from you that you want from them. Then everyone on the team receives a mutual benefit. You learn both to receive and give to each other. This fosters a warm, family feel that will take you through many a dark night in your journey to find your goals. The right people are out there. Maybe they are also looking for you, and when you find each other you can achieve your goals together. Be guardians for each other's lives, hearts, and souls.

Fuel Source No. 3: Relationships That Guard Your Dream

I serve on the boards of some nonprofit organizations whose missions I believe in. In a recent meeting of one of these boards, some of the leaders were discussing whether to change the organization's focus from serving its original target population to a group with a different demographic. Neither group was more deserving than the other; it was more a matter of evaluating the board's interest and the structure and fit of the organization to its beneficiaries.

I was surprised when one of the board members spoke up and said, "This organization was created to serve the population it is serving now. All of us signed on as board members because we felt a need to help these types of people. If we change the focus, we no longer serve the group I signed on to serve, and I'm out. I'll find an organization that helps the group I want to help." My first thought was, *It's not about you and what you want. It's about the organization.* I got the impression he wasn't truly interested in serving, but rather in pushing his own agenda. But then, the more I listened to him, the more I realized he was right. And I agreed with him. What had drawn all of us to helping out was that we felt something inside and had a personal investment in that particular set of people in need. We felt called to it, and we wanted to help the organization accomplish its mission because it fit with our own calling.

This man's comments helped refocus the original mission of the organization. In short, he served as a guardian of the dream. Things could have gone differently. We all could have agreed that our passions and callings had changed. Or we could have left and found another place to serve. Those options would have been okay. But in this situation, we kept our original focus, and the right thing for all was done.

You are the keeper of your dream. It is yours alone, and you hope it was birthed by God inside you. Its destiny is to grow and bear good and long-lasting fruit. But though it is your own dream, you must not guard it alone. You need people to stand with you who will join you in protecting and developing that dream. The relationships you need to find are people who will focus specifically on helping you achieve your goals. While your support team is guarding your life, this guardian team is about getting you to the success you want. That doesn't mean there can be no overlap between the two. Heart relationships and goal relationships can be the same. But achieving success generally takes people and teams, each of which is intentionally dedicated to only one of your tasks.

In choosing those who will serve as guardians of your dream, here are the two most important types of people you need to look for.

Peers in your area of interest. Find people who have experience and interest in your specific target area. If your desire is to pursue a graphic arts career, then talk to people who are headed in the same direction. Ask friends who they know. Do a World Wide Web search for people. Call businesses that are involved with graphic arts and ask if they have people or groups you can interact with. If your goal is more personal, for example, learning how to deal with emotional struggles, the process is the same. Call churches, counseling centers, and schools where there are people who have experience in these areas. Meet them and start asking questions. Whether it is a career or a problem, individuals in the same area of interest have a lot of knowledge about what you want to do. They can give you information, short cuts, and introduce you to other people who can help.

Coaches and mentors. This area has become its own industry in the last few years, and for good reason. Coaches and mentors have tremendous experience and competency in their areas of expertise. But just as importantly, they know how to teach, lead, and train others in those areas. To invest in a coaching relationship is to get a focused experience of growth that is tailored to your personal situation. It is highly intensive, provides a good return on investment, and can be a quantum leap for you.

My friend Jim is a man who certainly doesn't live for his work. He works so he can pay for his biking hobby. He is seriously into the sport, owning several bikes for different terrains, training for hours every week, and competing in century races (one hundred miles long) on weekends. This man is insane for his hobby.

Recently Jim wanted to go to the next level of ability, and to do that, he knew he needed a coach. He did some research and found the perfect person. She was a former Olympic cyclist, and her expertise was in working with guys like Jim—bikers who were good but wanted to get better. The only hitch was that this perfect person lived in another state. Jim found, however, that she coaches people all over the world through the Web and phone calls. He signed up with her and, after she got to know his background and goals, she provided him with a training schedule, a fitness regimen, and a diet plan tailored specifically for him. He worked the program. Within a couple of months, Jim was beating his own personal records and still improving at a significant rate. He has never met his coach face-to-face, nor does he think he ever will.

That is one of the differences between those who guard your life, and those who guard your dream. The "guard-your-life" support team really needs to be face-to-face for the personal contact, unless you are in some remote situation and it just isn't possible. The technical team, or "guard-your-dream" team (peers, coaches, and mentors) should ideally be face-to-face, but it is not as critical. More critical are aspects such as their knowledge base, experience, competency, and ability to convey the information.

Other Fuel Resources You Will Need

Connection isn't always about relationships. It is also about resources that will help you reach your goal, some of which people can provide, and some of which you can get in other ways. You need to plug into the external world of information and resources related to your goal. The idea is the same as in your people resources: *those who break out of the pack know they don't have it all inside their skin. They reach outside themselves for what they require.* Here are the principal types of external resources to look for:

Information. You need to know a lot of stuff to reach your dream. Be humble enough to admit your lack of knowledge. Only fools pretend to know things they don't, and they end up with less knowledge than anyone. People have been accomplishing great dreams for centuries, and they have amassed incredible amounts of valuable information along the way.

If you want to get a slim, athletic body, dig into the diet and exercise info. Become an expert in the field. If you want to run the company, read books on how others have done it. If you want the greatest marriage in the world, study the best thinkers and authors on the subject. Become an info junkie. Tons of information on every conceivable subject is out there just waiting to be tapped. You can find it in libraries, on the Web, in computer programs, in audio and video tapes, CDs, DVDs, and a host of other sources. The information you need is available. If you don't avail yourself of it, it's no one's fault but your own.

Several years ago, I read a magazine article featuring interviews of two of the best guitarists in the world. One of these virtuosos kept mentioning how much he was still a student of other people's techniques and artistry, and how much he learned from them—even from people who claim him as their own role model. The other guitarist spent a lot of time talking about how he was his own person, with his own style, and he didn't really gain a lot from other musicians because he listened exclusively to his own muse. The contrast was amazing. The interesting thing is that now, several years after that interview, you still hear the contributions and songs of the first guitarist, but the other one has fallen off the radar screen.

You don't have to re-invent the wheel. There is a treasure trove of information out there about exactly what you need to learn.

Training and experience. Information and knowledge are a good beginning, but they are not enough. People who reach their goals become skilled and experienced in their dream area. There is only one way for this to happen, and that is through training. Training puts the information to use in your mind and in your life. Don't stop with head knowledge.

People sometimes avoid the process of training and acquiring experience because it takes work, time, and forces them to admit failure. But there is no shortcut and no substitute. There is a saying: *Good judgment comes from experience; experience comes from bad judgment.* You had to fall off your bike a few times when you were little, but you learned to ride that way.

Training can be formal or informal, depending on your context. Coaches, mentors, and classes are the more structured and formal means. Their advantage is that the structure guarantees you certain experiences in a certain amount of time. Informal training can include volunteering to be a gofer for a coach whose sport you want to learn, or helping out at a service organization that provides assistance to the needy, or asking a friend in the insurance industry if you can shadow him for a day to see what his world is like. Generally, the informal training is more suited to finding whether you are interested in a particular area. When that is determined, you can move to a more structured experience.

Time and space. This resource is often harder to connect with than any other, but connect you must. People don't find their purpose in life on the fly or in off moments. *Achieving your success depends heavily on the time and space you allot to it.* And the exceptions to this principle are extremely rare, like maybe lottery winners. The reality is that most of the time the people who want to reach for better lives are already quite busy. They have jobs, relationships, families, and obligations, and those are all real and substantive responsibilities. These responsibilities and connections consume a lot of time, and it's hard to find the extra hours you need to advance your dream.

But it is doable. Every day people with full lives like you are moving step-by-step on an intentional path toward great goals. If others can do it, so can you. Here are some tips to help you.

- Trim the fat.

Put the next thirty days of your life on a calendar, either on a hard copy or on your computer. Write down all the essentials of your life, as well as the nonessentials that keep you balanced, such as social connections and hobbies. Then survey the entire month and evaluate your entries in light of their value to you when compared to your dream. You will often find some significant fat that you can trim off to allot more time to the goal.

- Farm it out.

Is there anything you are doing that you should let others do? Maybe you've been chairing a committee for many years, and it's time to step down. Can you work out a communal arrangement with other parents for taking each other's kids for an afternoon a week? Could a college kid do the tutoring of your child for you a couple of evenings a week? Can your spouse do more of the grocery shopping?

Sometimes we don't let go of tasks we're doing simply because we are control freaks. But more often than not, you'll be pleasantly surprised to find that when you farm out a task, the world doesn't fall apart. It was your own codependency that kept you locked in.

- Put the dream first.

When you have finished your calendar, put it aside and start over with a blank calendar. This time, your very first entries should be the blocks of time you need to get moving on your goal. Include such things as time for mentors, reading, training, and so on. Then arrange your life around those blocks of time and see if it works. Often people find that the important things still get done. This is similar to the financial savings principle in which, when you pay bills every month, the first person you pay is yourself (or, more specifically, your savings vehicle).

- Find your space.

Moving on your goals requires physical space that is yours alone, at least for adequate periods of time. You need an isolated place of your own in which you can brainstorm, dream, pray, and plan. These activities don't work well around kids, televisions, workplaces, or family activities. If absolutely no isolated space is available, you may need to tell everyone that you're holing up in the bedroom for a couple of hours, and you don't want to be interrupted. Or you may be able to go to the office after hours. Or even go to the library. Wherever it is, get a place where you can focus totally on working your plan.

- Get a friend to help.

Show your calendar to someone you trust—someone who manages time well and understands reality. Ask him or her to help you slash the time budget. A friend is likely to be more objective and able to see possibilities more clearly than you are, and that will help you do the necessary surgery on your time budget.

Feedback systems. Successful individuals generally adopt some sort of way to get information on how they are doing, monitor their progress, and see where they might be getting off track or out of balance. This is called a feedback system. Feedback systems can save you time and effort, keep you focused, or even improve your rate of progress. Coaches and friends are certainly part of that monitoring and feedback. But you can also set measurable goals (revenue, competency, weight loss, number of healthy dates per month) and periodically check your progress toward them.

For example, I have a simple Excel spreadsheet on my computer that has columns for the date, my weight, my workouts, my eating, my sleep hours, and comments about the day. It takes less than a minute each night to put in what I did that day. This little spreadsheet is a feedback system for my own physical health. Not only does it chart my progress, it also provides discipline. Knowing I will open it every day gives me a little more self-control. As the saying goes, that which is observed tends to improve. Feedback systems help you observe yourself in reaching your dream.

As you can see, there are lots of resources out there, and they are designed to propel you to success. People who are into ownership are always on the lookout for more resources, because they understand their value.

As we said at the beginning of this section, you need to find the fuel. And you find it by connecting to the right resources. But that is not enough; finding the fuel is just one part of the story here. The next step is to know how to burn the fuel. Learning to burn the fuel efficiently will propel you that much closer to your dream. If it just sits there in your tank, it's dead weight. The next section will help you use the resources you find.

BURN THE FUEL

I have known many people who are no different from anyone else wanting a better life. They are bright, talented, and goodhearted. But often they don't reach their goals because they don't know how to use the resources they have. They are connected to the right people and places, but they don't get the results they want. You can avoid this failure and maximize your resources with the following recommendations. They are simple, but they work for people who are on their way to achievement.

Invite the feedback from your life guardians. You can pretty much assume that your goal guardians—those experts you tap for specialized information—know they need to give you helpful feedback. That's automatically built into what you go to them for. But with close friends who are part of your feedback system, things are different. Don't make the mistake of assuming that they also know you need their input. They may think that all you want from them is encouragement, acceptance, and grace. They may also think that if you want feedback on something specific, you'll ask for it. Often your friends just don't want to sound critical or hurt your feelings, and you can't blame them for that.

But you don't want to miss out on the tremendous help and value these people can bring to you. Your life guardians—as opposed to your goal guardians—can give you advice, insight, ideas, corrections, and confrontations that can literally make all the difference in the world to your goal.

When you are creating your support team, be sure to give each person permission to tell you the truth, not only with love and support, but also with directness and clarity. They may not at first believe you are serious. So when they venture out and say something like, "Well, I've noticed that you seem to waste a lot of time blaming others for your lack of progress," you need to say, "Thank you for that correction. May I please have another?" After they see that you didn't curl up into the fetal position or get defensive or act out a victim role, they will begin to tell you realities that can protect and enhance your growth. That is, if they are the right people for your team.

Keep resources separate from the outcome. You will inevitably get close to your resource people, certainly to the life guardians, and often to the dream guardians as well. A sense of connectedness is a natural result when people open up their lives to each other over time. And that's a good thing. Keep in mind, however, that no matter how valuable these people are to you, the final outcome is your responsibility, not theirs. This is your dream, and you need to stay in ownership of it. There is often a temptation to let the team share the burden. Some sharing is helpful, but their role is really to support and assist you. If you stumble or fail, you must take responsibility for it and repair the situation. It's not their fault when you fail. The outcome is yours.

It's a little like a company that tries to be so democratic that no one at all is in authority. It seems ideally equal and cooperative until there is a problem. If no one is in charge, then no one is responsible. "We are all responsible" doesn't lend itself to cleaning up messes. President Harry Truman's "the buck stops here" accurately defines your responsibility for your dream. That slogan is worth adopting as your own.

Be grateful, open, and nondefensive. Be thankful every day for the people in your life who have signed up on a volunteer or professional level to walk with you toward your dream. They are a tremendous gift. The more you appreciate their contributions, the better you will utilize the wisdom and help they offer you. Be open to what they tell you, and never get into power struggles with them. Try their suggestions, even if at first they don't seem to make sense. Certainly you should question and challenge, but remember that you probably need to listen to these people more than talk.

When Jesus taught, trained, and resourced people, he said lots of things that either made no sense to them or were highly confrontive:

- When Peter wanted to prevent Jesus' death, Jesus said, "Get behind Me, Satan."[1]

- He told the disciples that the way to save their lives was to lose them.[2]

- He told Nicodemus he must be born twice, which totally confuses him.[3]

- When people wanted to know when the kingdom of God was coming, he told them it was within them.[4]

- When people wanted a miracle, he told them that he would rebuild the temple in three days, but he wasn't referring to a literal temple.[5]

- He said that being sad could be a good thing for people.[6]

Yet today the words of Jesus still bring illumination, insight, and help to all areas of people's lives, if they truly have ears to hear. Successful people don't mind being confused by their mentors. It is just another step in the path of learning and growing. Be open to what you hear from your guardians, even if at first it doesn't go down very well.

Normalize complexity and different viewpoints. One of the greatest ways to burn your fuel efficiently is to normalize, or become comfortable with, complex situations, answers, and varying viewpoints you encounter from your resources. You need the ability not to feel derailed or overwhelmed by gray areas and ambiguity, for that is the way life really is.

Most meaningful goals and dreams, and most of our most challenging problems, have several levels of complexity and more than one approach to addressing them. It is tempting to simplify and look for the one right way or the three steps to get you there. But that is a child's way of organizing the world. Grownups don't want to have reality digested into an easily swallowed capsule, for the reduction process may dump needed information. They want the feedback or perspective even if the subject is so complex that various people advising them disagree with each other. Sorting through competing options can be one of the most helpful experiences you will have. Having to make the choice yourself will assist you in taking responsibility for your path, your progress, and your outcome.

A friend of mine assessed his financial situation in relation to his current job, and he was dismayed to find that if things did not change, he would not be able to retire at his targeted age. He went into a research mode to determine the yearly income he needed from that point on. It was more than his current position would generate, but he liked his job and didn't want to leave it. So he searched for ways to supplement his income.

Eventually he found a part-time business that wouldn't take too much of his time because it generated passive income. (An example of passive income would be interest on a savings account.) Before he plunged, however, he resourced financial experts, successful people in that industry, insurance people, accounting people, and other pertinent sources of information. The resulting data was quite complex. The experts' recommendations were not all consistent with each other, and they addressed several different levels of his situation. In addition, all these people represented different industries and used different terms and almost different languages. It was highly confusing for a while, but he stayed on the learning curve and committed himself to making sense of all the opinions. In a short time, he became more conversant with what all the experts were saying, and he was able to pick and choose what he needed from their input. He is now well on the way to meeting his financial goals. He still consults with his experts, because now he knows how to use them in the way that furthers his own dream.

Don't be afraid of complexity and conflicting advice. Listen, learn, and you will soon be able to equip yourself with the information and experiences you need.

Connecting Will Bear Good Fruit for You

It is not good to be alone, especially when you are stretching your life and working hard to achieve a cherished goal. You need to connect. It is far better to reach out and find the people, the information, and the experiences that will empower you to take the next step, and to make sure it is the right step.

6

You Can Learn to Say No

6

Any occurrence requiring undivided attention
will be accompanied by a compelling distraction.
—ROBERT BLOCH

One of the most inspirational stories in recent years is that of Team Hoyt, the athletic partnership of father-and-son Dick and Rick Hoyt of Massachusetts.

Over the past twenty-five years, the two have competed as a team in over two hundred triathlons and sixty-four marathons. In 1992, they biked and ran across the entire United States in forty-five consecutive days. This is an astounding record by any measure. What raises Team Hoyt to a different level entirely, however, is the fact that since birth, Rick Hoyt has been a spastic quadriplegic with cerebral palsy who is also unable to speak. How these two men have achieved what they have is a great lesson for all of us who wish to achieve great goals and dreams in our own lives.

When Rick was born to Dick and Judy Hoyt, the umbilical cord coiled around his neck, cutting off oxygen to his brain. The doctors told the young parents that Rick would be profoundly intellectually disabled all his life. The two did not want to accept that news, however, and determined to raise their son as normally as possible. They began family life with that attitude, and over the years added two more sons to the mix.

As time went on, Dick and Judy began seeing signs that Rick was as intelligent as his brothers. The school authorities didn't believe this, and so they resisted the family's efforts to get Rick accepted into public school. A group of engineers from Tufts University met Rick. As they were interacting with him they told him a joke and he cracked up. This led the engineers to believe that Rick could understand concepts and communicate. That inspired them to create an interactive computer, which Rick could use to communicate thoughts with head movements. Once Rick was trained on the computer, it became clear that he possessed normal intelligence. At age thirteen Rick was admitted to public school.

When Rick was fifteen, a local five-mile benefit run was planned to raise support for a local lacrosse player who had been paralyzed in an accident. Rick wanted to participate, so Dick pushed his son in his wheelchair in their first race. Though they finished next to last, Rick told his dad that when they competed he no longer felt handicapped, but normal. This experience was so positive for them that the two began entering more races and clocking better and better times. In 1981, they finished their first Boston Marathon in the top quarter of the field.

Rick went on to graduate from Boston University and now works at Boston College, helping to develop ways that a paralyzed person can control mechanical aids, such as powered wheelchairs by eye movements. And in addition to keeping up their race schedule, Team Hoyt also conducts motivational speaking tours to audiences across the country.

Over the years, the two have brought hope and inspiration to many thousands of people.[1]

Put yourself in the Hoyts' shoes for a moment. They had a dream, as you do, which has the potential for accomplishing great good on many levels. Imagine also the huge obstacles they faced and learn from their determination to say *no* to those obstacles.

For one thing, Dick worked full time, and the couple had three kids, so there wasn't a lot of extra time and money floating around. They had to say *no* to the idea that their dream wasn't possible. Another obstacle was Rick's condition, which required a great deal of effort and maintenance. They had to say *no* to discouragement and resignation. Add to that the fact that no one had ever done anything like this; and there was no model, no instruction manual, no precedent. They had to say *no* to fears of the unknown. And also, during the early days they encountered a great deal of social resistance to the idea of their competing as a team. Other athletes would shun them at races. They had to say *no* to criticism and negative feedback. (Fortunately, such attitudes in the athletic world are much changed for the better in recent years.) Yet Dick and Rick are a success; they have achieved, and are still achieving, great goals.

One aspect of Team Hoyt's example can help you take control of your life and reach your goals. The principle is to *say* no *to anything that would divert you from your goals and dreams.* This power comes by skill, training, and effort, and it is invaluable in your endeavors. The idea of saying *no* may seem negative, but if you say no to the right things, it has a very positive outcome. It's easy to blame circumstances and the bad hand you were dealt and say, *It's not my fault.* But it's thousands of times more rewarding to say no to those things that stand in your way and play your hand to win.

All of us must say *yes* to all the other principles we have presented in this book, such as owning our lives and choices, facing failure, persisting, changing our thinking, stretching, and connecting. But those *yeses* aren't enough. A *no* is also necessary—a very special and specific kind of *no*.

We need to protect and guard our dream from forces that might prevent us from reaching what we want to reach. We need to learn the skill of saying no to those forces. Just as every successful sports team requires both offense and defense, so do you. In this chapter, we give you the defense strategy to keep you on task, on goal, and protected. You will need it.

Be a Guardian

First, take another look at the center of your motivation—the goal you want to achieve. Is your goal pursuing a better career path? Renewing a marriage or recharging a dating life? Solving a bad habit? Improving a family situation? Getting in shape? Whatever your dream, it is more than just a "head" thing, or some intellectual, cognitive awareness. It goes deeper than that. It is a matter of the heart.

People don't invest time, effort, sweat, and money in things that are just head issues. They become involved when something reaches their heart. The heart is where we live, find purpose, meaning, and fulfillment. It is where we truly understand what really matters most to us. It is what keeps us up at night, drives us to learn about the idea, and keeps us praying for guidance and success. All great dreams begin in the heart, with a vision, a goal, or a plan.

At the same time, the dream you carry within your heart is fragile and young. It is not yet a fully realized, mature reality. It is a dream. It is a seed that has been planted within you and is slowly taking root. It is starting to grow. But it needs time, support, experience, and help to become what it should be: a new company, a loving relationship, a victory over an addiction, or a way to best utilize your own gifts and talents in life. Especially in the early germination stage of your dream, you need to be a guardian, one who protects and supports the development of what is to be. You need to be watchful and vigilant to make sure that the goal within is not overwhelmed, injured, or neglected. You are your dream's first and best defense.

You may find yourself somewhat put off by this idea. To some, self-protection sounds selfish and "all about me." And certainly we are capable of great self-centeredness and narcissism, which are never good things. But that is not what we are talking about here. Self-protection as we're presenting the idea is more about stewardship, not selfishness. Your life, heart, and dreams are ideally things which you should use to be a better person, to help others in some way, to make the world a better place, and to advance the kingdom of God in your given field. They are about the fact that you have a responsibility to invest your life, talents, and gifts in a way that makes sense of the purpose for which you were placed on the earth.

So don't be afraid to set a fence of protection around your heart. You are executing ownership and stewardship. I love the way that King Solomon, the wise man, said it: "Above all else, guard your heart, for it affects everything you do" (Proverbs 4:23 NLT). Your heart possesses your dream. When you guard your heart, you protect your dream.

THE ZONE

Nobody takes ownership and makes great life changes on the fly. If you could have transformed your life, work, and relationships in your extra time between errands, you would already have done it long before now. Life and change just don't work that way. Achieving the things we desire most will always require a period of extended space and time for you to dream, learn, plan, and risk. The process needs to be calendared and safeguarded. It helps us to get into the *zone*—that mental state in which you are totally focused on whatever stage of your dream you are working on. It's a temporary period of concentration in which you apply all your thoughts and energies to the dream. The time you spend in your zone can be extremely effective.

People get into zones in all phases of life. It's as though time stands still. An NBA player will be unstoppable and score forty points; it's as though he cannot miss. A salesman will have a series of great deals go through, and when asked how he did it, he will say, "I don't know, I was just hot this month." Members of a support group will have a meeting in which they open up, become vulnerable to each other, and find that the time passes as if it were no time at all. A person working on a career plan will spend a Thursday morning creating and plotting and suddenly realize that it's already lunchtime. You need to create and protect zone times for yourself. When you make these a normal part of life, you will be amazed at the speed of your progress.

But let's not forget about those protective *nos*. Before you can reach your zone you must be aware of, mindful of, and prepared to say no to several obstacles.

Obstacles to the Zone: Distractions

First, start paying attention to those things and activities that distract you from your steps toward your goal. They don't have to be negative or unhealthy things at all. In fact, they can be very good for you. That's probably why they distract you. But even good things can impede your efforts to get moving and finish the race. They can slow your momentum, get you sidetracked, and stall you.

Information Age Incursions: The phenomenal Information Age we live in is both a blessing and a curse. You can find facts and contact people in incredibly short periods of time, and that can be a great advantage to work and relationships. But at the same time, those same technological advances give others access to you at any given moment. Your land-line phone rings. Your cell phone chimes. Your e-mail alert chirps. Your fax machine lands a copy. An instant message pops up on your computer monitor (I wondered why my kids weren't getting their homework done in time until I saw them trying to do online research while keeping four or five instant message conversations going at the same time!). And to top it all off, this is no longer limited to the office or even the home. PDAs and mobile phones make it possible for others to access you almost anywhere on the globe at any time.

Then there are the type of Information Age distractions that aren't about others getting to us, but more about us getting lured away from our tasks by piddling stuff that seems so easy and accessible that we think little of it. Things like Web browsing, low-priority e-mails, and unnecessary phone calls. A vast world of people and information are only a click or a dial away nowadays, and all too often we yield to the temptation to connect when we should protect our dream and say no.

Most of us cope with these distractions as normal parts of life and work, which to a large extent, they are. But when you are embarking on a personal mission, the kind we are talking about in this book, these distractions can be a significant problem. When your goal in life is merely to make it to 5 p.m. so you can have dinner and watch

TV, the Information Age distractions are not a problem, for you have nothing to be distracted from. But the fact that you're reading this book is a strong indication that this is not you. You've got to get control of your distractions, because they work against your ability to get into your life transformation zone.

One thing that can help immensely is to get rid of an insidious false expectation thrust upon us by electronic communications. We are now trained to think that *because others have access to us, we are obliged to respond to them.* It sounds crazy, but it is true. Most of us tend to feel that just because someone sent an e-mail or left a voice-mail message, we are responsible to give an instant response. And some people do expect that. How many times have you heard something like, "I e-mailed you this morning; why haven't you responded?" or "I left you a voice-mail an hour ago; why didn't you answer?" Now, just who is in charge of your dream?

Remember that you owe people what you have promised to owe people, not what they expect because they left you a message. Get out of the guilt trap here. It will never lead you to your new life. Sometimes when I work at the computer, I turn off my e-mail program so I won't be tempted to answer everything that pops up. And I also leave the phone off, except for patient emergency contingencies, and pick up voice-mail a couple of times a day—just so I can be free from distractions in my work.

Try this exercise: One day this week, keep a record of how many conversations, e-mails, voice-mails, instant messaging, and so on you dealt with. Note which ones were about survival, which ones helped you in your dream, and which ones were nice but unnecessary and took time from your dream. You will probably be surprised at how much of an investment you make in unnecessary calls and responses. That is valuable time you can put to better use. Use your time log as a basis for making decisions as to what communication distractions you will say no to in order to accomplish your dream.

Other Distractions. But Information Age distractions aren't the only ones to be aware of. Evaluate activities such as TV watching, goofing off periods, idle conversations, and over-organizing. All of these activities have their place and can serve us well, but if not controlled they can also siphon off time and energy. The good news is that the simple act of evaluating and measuring how much time you spend on these things will almost certainly put them in better balance.

Most distractions are reduced when we pay attention to them and increased when we don't think about them. Get in charge of your time by saying no to distractions. And when you make a significant amount of progress toward your goal, celebrate by giving in to some of them in measured doses.

Obstacles to the Zone: Toxic People

When I was in my early years of training as a psychologist, I asked a more experienced psychologist to meet with me and advise me on counseling matters. He was helpful in several cases I was dealing with. But one day I described a very difficult situation with a tough client, and he said, "Give it up, he'll never get better."

"What do you mean?" I said.

"He's been that way too long," he replied. "He'll never change."

He had said similar things about other clients, and I became bothered by these statements. If he was right, what was I doing in this business? I just couldn't see how he could say that anyone was hopeless. It didn't square with what I had learned in school, or with my own personal experience, or with what I knew about the power of

God's grace and healing. I did a lot of soul-searching, and I realized that this was not the stance I wanted to take in this profession. I drove myself to study more about the particular issue my problem client was dealing with, I got supervision from other therapists, and I stopped seeing the one who advised me to write off difficult cases. The result was that my client began making significant improvements in his life. I just had to quarantine myself from a toxic person who was giving me unhelpful and untrue advice.

I guarantee you that alongside your dream, goal, or problem will come a toxic person or two. By "toxic person" I mean someone who has a negative influence on the direction of your desires. A simple conversation with a toxic person can leave you discouraged, feeling like a failure, confused, or even questioning your dream. Toxic people sap the energy, drive, and passion you require to continue making progress.

This isn't to say that you don't need confrontive, corrective people in your life. As we said in chapter 5 on connecting, direct and healthy feedback from those who are for us is vitally helpful. It's not the negative statements that are the problem, for sometimes negative truths help. *The problem with toxic people is the negative outcomes that they produce in our minds.* You must learn to say no to the following types of toxic people:

Envious People. There are certain folks who get a weird joy out of the failure of others and are bothered by others' success. Deep within these people beats an envious heart. Though they would never admit it, they feel quite empty inside, and they resent the perceived good fortune of others. However, they resist the effort it takes for them to achieve that good fortune. So in sick ways, they are dream destroyers, saying things like "So you think going to grad school will make you better than everybody else?" or "Oh, you're losing weight; I didn't know you were that desperate for a man," or "I see you're working for a promotion; bet you have to kiss up a lot." The toxic nature of these comments is often hidden under the guise of kidding around, but the attack is there. When you fail in achieving your success, they feel better about their own failures.

Quarantine these dream destroyers! If you have an envious person in your life, confront him and tell him you don't need that in the relationship. Tell him that you need someone who is on your team and who believes in your goal. And if he continues, keep some distance between him and your dream. Don't even bring up the subject, and change the subject if he brings it up. Remember that you are the only guardian your dream has.

Negative People. While we said that negative feedback can be a positive thing, there are some people who are simply negative about everything, and they produce negative fruit in our lives. They see only the dark side of everything, and nothing seems hopeful. They may say, for example, "You and Jason won't make it; I just don't think the relationship will last," or "I've tried to go to a gym, too, and I can tell you, you'll give it up after a while," or "The boss never listens to anybody, so why go to the trouble?" Often they feel negative about their own lives as well, and that is a sad thing. But you can't let their poison overflow into your dream.

It's hard enough to maintain positive hope in working for your vision. It takes its toll in time, work, risk, and failure. The last thing you need is someone who echoes whatever fears and negative thoughts may already be running around in your head! Tell your friend, "I am really excited about my new goal, and I need hopefulness and encouragement from you. If you have a real and true negative thing to say about it that can help me identify and overcome an obstacle,

I want to hear it. But it's not okay if all I hear from you is the hopelessly negative. Can you give me a good balance? That would really help." Often, a negative person won't even be aware of his tendency and will make the correction.

Controlling People. Be aware of certain people who really do want you to fulfill a dream. The only problem is that it's *their* dream they want you to achieve, not yours! They are called controlling people. These types tend to see people as means to their own ends. And generally, relationships with these people go well when others live life their way. But if you peel off and follow your own star, they resist the move and become toxic.

For example, a husband may not want his wife to enter the workforce even when the kids are old enough to be relatively independent, because she won't be around to keep him comfortable. A co-worker may be competitive with you in the job and attempt to run things his way. Or a woman may not want her date to have other female friends because he may be attracted to someone else. If you find yourself in this sort of relationship, nip it in the bud. Say, "Our relationship is important to me. But it seems to me that when we do things that mean a lot to you, all goes well, but when I try to bring in things I like, they don't go well. I need for this relationship to be mutual, and I need your support when I make choices of my own. Those choices aren't choices *against* us; they are *for* me. I am glad you have your preferences. But this relationship needs to go both ways." Insist on mutual freedom.

Needy People. People on the go often have dependent relationships that they don't know what to do with. These are individuals who, for any number of reasons, have tremendous life struggles and challenges and often deal with grave problems. They are needy and ask for a great deal of time, energy, and support. You may find yourself functioning as someone's life support system. For example, you may have a friend who is going through a divorce and calls often for advice and a listening ear. Or you could have someone who has lost a job and is trying to pick up the pieces. Sometimes a needy person has a long history of failure and crisis and has for years been dependent on others to take care of him.

A needy person is often a very good person who is not truly toxic at heart. He may simply be going through his own dark night of the soul, as do all of us at some point in life. Or he may have a dependent character issue that prevents him from being autonomous and in charge. Though a needy person may be good hearted, his impact on you and your aspirations may have the outcome of being toxic and a distraction from your path.

It is important to realize that most needy people truly need help, support, time, and encouragement. They often benefit greatly from a community that connects with them to give them safety and stability. We are all called to reach out to the needy and give back what has been given to us. That is a large part of what life is all about. As the biblical proverb says, "Speak up and judge fairly; defend the rights of the poor and needy" (Proverbs 31:9 NIV). So if you have a dependent relationship in your life, make sure that you are being generous, sacrificing, and caring for that person.

At the same time, however, be certain that what you are doing is actually what is best for him. It is easy to think that being totally available to struggling individuals is what they need. Sometimes that is true. For example, if you have a child who is very ill or has a serious problem, a great deal of life must go on the back burner so that you can give him the time and resources he needs. Or your friend in a marital nightmare may, for a season of life, call on you often to keep her existence together. Helping those with needs such as these can be right, loving, proper, and good. In fact, for some people, that ability to help the needy is their true calling. Mother Teresa is a wonderful example. Meeting the desperate needs of others puts those people in their right place. For others, helping the afflicted coexists with and is supported by their own desire to grow, change, and achieve.

But it's important to be aware that sometimes a needy person needs more than we can provide. That is not his fault; it is just the reality of his situation. You may not have the expertise to meet his needs that a good church, counselor, pastor, support group, or financial expert might provide. If that is the case, become a conduit for help, rather than the sole source of care. You may help that individual better by being a bridge to what is really needed. If your friend is hemorrhaging, it may not be your job to be the surgeon, but rather the ambulance that gets him to the surgeon. Also, bear in mind that in crises, the early stages are generally more demanding than the latter ones. In the beginning, you may need to spend more time and energy until your friend is stabilized and able to walk better on his own.

So do not turn your back on the needy. Be there for them in the best ways that you can help. And as you give what you can truly provide, be sure that you also guide them to resources and structures that can help them on their own path. And continue taking steps down your own path.

Obstacles to the Zone: The Worthy-but-Untimely

I was consulting with the president of a small but profitable company who felt that his job was eating him up. It was requiring too much time and energy, and he was afraid he was headed for burn-out. As we talked, however, it became clear to me that the job itself wasn't the problem.

What I began to uncover was the fact that this man was taking on projects and new business opportunities that were getting in the way of his primary focus and mission. He was a very positive and expansive person, and these attributes contributed to his situation. When a proposal with good potential to take off and boost revenues came across his desk, he got excited about it and immediately assigned himself either to spearhead the project or oversee someone who could (not realizing that overseeing also takes time and energy).

After I realized what was going on, I said, "It's not really the job. The real problem is that you have a hard time perceiving that some things can be worthy and yet untimely."

"What do you mean?" he asked.

"Well," I said, "these opportunities you are looking at right now seem really viable to me. I think they are worthy. They are projects your company could do well, and they could be highly profitable. And if your company was larger and had more resources, you should definitely be investing in them. But they aren't timely. They don't fit where you are at this time of your company's life. The resources you have to siphon off to get them off the ground will cost too much to the bread and butter business you're already handling. And what's worse, this diffusion of resources could cause your organization to go backwards and even lose its cutting edge."

He hated to hear that. Such an energetic and forward-thinking guy really doesn't like to lose opportunities. But he did listen, and he began to let some great deals go so he could stay on track. And eventually the company grew under his leading and was able to take on more. An even bigger plus was that as he said *no* to worthy but untimely opportunities, he also experienced more personal freedom, less stress, and more satisfaction in the job. Basically, he cut out everything that wasn't the job and just started doing the job again. I have seen the opposite happen over and over in the lives of people who are moving toward visionary goals. They make good progress toward their goal, and then out of the blue come these fantastic extra opportunities. They become distracted, veer off course, and lose momentum toward their dream.

Of course, sometimes that unexpected new opportunity should be seized. When a Web-based company that was born in a garage receives a nine-figure buyout offer within a couple of years of its inception, it could very well be time to take the offer and change course. But most of the time, you should look long and hard at the good new things on the horizon. Do they fit your vision? Will they steer you away or toward it? Are they worthy but untimely?

This is also true in other areas of life. You might be concentrating on your personal growth, engaged in activities such as joining a support group, reading self-help literature, journaling, having lunch with people who are into growth and change, and working to improve yourself and your relationships. Then suddenly you are asked to lead a couple of groups just because people find out that you are good at that. Plus you are asked to get more involved in the company's HR activities. And pretty soon, you have to back off from the vision because of all the worthy-but-untimely activities. Or suppose you are a single woman who finally develops a close dating relationship with a man you can connect with, and things become exclusive between the two of you. Then, wham! Three other really super guys suddenly show up!

Letting go of the worthy-but-untimely is not easy. Losing potentially good experiences is a real loss. But my experience in working with successful people is that when they reach a goal, they find many other opportunities waiting for them. Successful, dream-reaching people who own their lives will always have other people wanting their time, expertise, and leadership. You've got to learn to say no to the appropriate people and situations.

Obstacles to the Zone: Your Own Codependency

You probably knew that even in a book about dreams and goals, the word *codependency* would have to appear when the authors are a couple of psychologists! But codependency has got to be addressed because it can become a huge obstacle in your path to success. And this chapter is the place to address it because learning to say no is crucial to removing this obstacle.

Codependency is most simply defined as a tendency to take too much responsibility for the problems of others. While it's good to care for, help, and support people, the codependent crosses a line in the relationship—*the line of responsibility.* Instead of being responsible *to* others, the codependent becomes responsible *for* them. And, unless the other person is your child or someone whose care is entrusted to you, the line of responsibility between the *to* and the *for* can become quite blurred. The result is that instead of caring and helping, you begin enabling and rescuing. Enabling and rescuing do not empower anybody. They only increase dependency, entitlement, and irresponsibility. Love builds up strength and character, whereas codependency breaks them down.

Codependency unchecked can take you right off the rails of your goals and dreams. And it's all too easy to be completely unaware of it. This is because while distractions, toxic people, and worthy-but-untimely things are outside of you, codependency is *within* you.

Sometimes it is just too close to see. But it is there, at least in small part, in most of us.

For example, you are late to your night class in the MBA track because a co-worker drops the ball and asks you to work late to bail him out. Or you want to take sailing lessons, but your wife doesn't like to try new things and prefers to stay at home and watch television. Since she feels lonely when you are gone, you stay home, which actually ends up being worse for the both of you. Or perhaps you feel guilty for the fact that all your efforts at online dating are paying off, while your girlfriends are moping and complaining about their lack of prospects. So you hide your success from them, or even slow down the process.

Most of the time, the problem centers on the unhappiness of the other person. Since we care about him, we don't want him to be sad, hurt, disappointed, or unhappy. And that kind of care is a good thing. However, no one has ever yet made an unhappy person happy. You can't take the emotions of another person and change them for her. You can help, love, accept, empathize, advise, challenge, confront, and support. But at the end of the day, her feelings belong to her. So you must say *no* to enabling and rescuing behaviors. Life gets better and people become more successful when they are able to shoulder their own responsibilities: "For each one should carry his own load."[2]

When you start saying *no* to your own codependency, however, you will also find yourself saying *no* to people you have been rescuing. So be ready for some twinges of guilt. You may feel like the bad guy or fear that the other person will think badly of you. These feelings are normal; consider them part of the price of reaching your dreams. Just remember to stay loving and caring while respecting the line of responsibility. The guilty feelings should resolve in time, and you will become a freer person.

EXCUSES

We have discussed the problem of making excuses in other parts of this book, but it is simply too important not to include in this chapter. If you intend to get in control and take ownership of your dreams, *you must say* no *to all excuses you have been making.* Excuses may exist in any form, from blaming others, to minimizing your contributions, to rationalizing, to outright denials of your responsibility. Excuses are not your friend; they are your enemy. They cause you to dismiss your lack of progress as not being your own fault, but rather the fault of others or of circumstances.

Take a zero tolerance stance with your excuses. An excuse is its own reward, but the satisfaction that it brings is fleeting. It acts as an anesthetic. It may temporarily medicate the pain of your unfulfilled dreams, but when the effect wears off, your situation has not improved and, what is worse, time has been passing you by. Time is a commodity that simply cannot be replaced or remade, so you can't afford to lose any of it to your excuses.

What are the best ways to say *no* to this dream-killer called excuse? Here are a few tips that can help you put it to rest:

Put your excuses in writing. Write down on paper the excuses that have kept you from moving ahead: "I'm too busy," "I don't have enough support," "I didn't have the advantages that others have," "Someone in my life holds me back," and all the rest. When you've made your list, then write down where these excuses came from. Remember that most of the time excuses are a product of fear. For example, "I am afraid of failure," "I am uncomfortable with the unknown," "I don't want to risk negative reactions from others," "I fear that I am a loser," or "I am afraid of getting excited and then being let down." Admitting the fear is a sign of ownership and progress. Once you admit your fears, you can own and confront them. You cannot own and confront anything when you make excuses.

Then add another part to your writing. Record what your excuses have cost you in your life. What price have you paid for the anesthetic? Lost job opportunities? Earnings over a lifetime? A more loving and passionate marriage? A successful dating life? Ways to develop your gifts and talents? This list may be hard to make, but it will help you to crystallize within your mind the reality that a life of excuses must now be over for you.

Get accountability partners. Show your excuse list to a few safe, loving, and honest friends. Ask them to check in with you as you work toward your goal. Give them permission to tell you when they hear you making excuses again. You don't want them to be judgmental or harsh. But have them point out the old excuse language when you use it, so you can catch it and deal with it. And the sooner the better.

Be aware of the seasons of ownership. Timing is important in saying *no* to excuses. When you first start tackling your problem or planning your goal, you are less likely to use excuses. The honeymoon period is exciting, full of energy, and somewhat removed from reality, as it should be. The beginning euphoria and enthusiasm serves to launch you toward your vision. But after the honeymoon, you will encounter the obstacles that have always stopped you: certain people, your circumstances, or some handicapping attitude of your own.

This is when you need to be alert to the excuses and be ready to terminate them. When you or your friends hear an excuse come from your mouth, such as "I can't do that because if I fail it would let everyone down," simply step above the excuse so you can see it clearly for what it is. Recognize it as an excuse, admit that it came from a fear, and clarify the reality of it by restating the fear in a way that identifies it for what it is. "I just got afraid that I would let everyone down." Now you can own the fear and the response to it. This enables you to put it behind you, to get the assurance, courage, and strengthening you need to move on. Remember the power of receiving affirmation and encouragement in times of stress and doubt: "So encourage each other and build each other up." (1 Thessalonians 5:11 NLT). Excuses require confrontation. Ownership requires validation.

Experience the results of ownership. Excuses are their own reward, but they are unsatisfying, short-lived rewards. Ownership, on the other hand, creates rewards worth having. As you move out of the avoidance of risk that excuses bring and enter a lifestyle of ownership and initiative, you will begin to experience movement toward your goal. It may be only a little at a time, but celebrate those small victories. They will help you continue day by day until winning the skirmishes leads to victory in the battles.

For example, perhaps you have never been able to talk effectively to your spouse about working on the marriage together. Perhaps every time you tried he shut you down or withdrew or the attempt escalated into a huge fight. You're tempted to fall back on your fear-based excuse for not trying anymore: "It never does any good, and the blowup it causes is just too hard to deal with." Instead of the excuse, try another approach: "I know this is difficult for you to hear, and I am sorry that I haven't brought it up in the right ways, but I want something better for us than what we have. I love you, but I'm not happy with what our relationship has become. And I am going to insist that we both work on the marriage. This is very important to me, and I am not going to let it go. I want to hear what I am doing that makes things harder for you. And I want you to hear my view also. When can we have a conversation about this?"

You may get silence or denial or anger. But you will know that you spoke directly, lovingly, and clearly. This is a first step. This is progress, and you should tell your support team about it and have a party as you get ready for the next step.

Not Settling for Less

In 1960 Richard Nixon ran for president of the United States against John F. Kennedy. Nixon was defeated. In 1968, he ran for president against Hubert Humphrey. This time Nixon won. Regardless of what you think of his politics, Nixon performed an incredible feat in rising from defeat to achieve the most coveted political position in the world. It took great effort, perseverance, and forethought to accomplish this unheard-of dream. Nixon refused to settle for less than what he truly desired. For those who are learning the skill of ownership and success, Nixon's example is a great teacher in saying *no* to settling for less.

When we encounter obstacles to our dream, we all have a tendency to surrender ownership by resigning ourselves to lesser goals. It's the path of least resistance. It's always tempting to lower the bar to a level that is more reachable, that takes less effort, and that causes less stress. But what happens when we settle for something that we really didn't shoot for? Often a nagging question eats at us: *What if I had stayed with the original dream?*

Suppose, for example, your goal is to lose fifty pounds. You drop ten pounds, twenty, and twenty-five, but then you have a real struggle at thirty. The pounds come off slower, the appetite returns, and working out becomes drudgery. It is only natural to want to stop and say, "Hey, losing thirty pounds is not all that bad." You are certainly much better off than you were before you began. But ask yourself: are you stopping because it's the best path for you, or because you are settling? It might be far better instead to change things in the diet and regimen, talk to a specialist, or join a group. A plateau does not have to be the end of the line.

Or suppose that you have a goal to reach a certain position in your field within the next two years, and you don't quite get there. Should you be grateful for the progress you have made and stop where you are? Or is it time to unpack your life with a consultant and see why you are stalled?

Or suppose you have an adolescent who is getting into trouble with alcohol, drugs, and legal problems. Your original goal might have been that he graduate from high school and be accepted at a college. But as tough as that is these days, perhaps you will be happy if he just becomes drug-free and let it go at that.

There is no doubt that some goals need to be adjusted for reasons of reality and good judgment. Some dreams weren't realistic to begin with. Some require mid-course changes as new factors arise. Michael Jordan is, in the minds of most people, the best player in NBA history. However, he failed in his next goal—to enter the world of major league baseball when he tried it in 1994. He wisely left that sport and returned to basketball, where he once again became the best. Jordan simply accepted reality and adjusted his goals accordingly.

Before you get ready to settle and modify your goal, however, you need to make sure of one thing: *be sure that you are accepting true reality rather than avoiding failure.* Many people stop before they really need to because the threat of failing is too painful, too shameful, or too disappointing. Rather than saying, "I didn't make the dream," they cover their failure by saying, "I just made myself a different dream." This is nothing but a rationalization—and a real dream killer.

Here is a better approach: *learn to take the sting out of failure.* Ultimately, what's wrong with saying you failed? Nothing at all. And furthermore, there is a great deal right about it. When you admit failure, you can learn from it. You can analyze your failure and find out what went wrong the first time around. You can try different approaches. You can get new input from people and resources around you. You can get a fresh start. You can get ready to try, and fail, and try, and fail, and try again.

So say *no* to settling for less and never knowing what your potential could have been. Refuse to live in the land of regrets, where no one ever really tried. Instead, enter the land of high goals, where you ultimately cannot lose.

The Robert Bloch quote at the beginning of this chapter applies to us all: *Any occurrence requiring undivided attention will be accompanied by a compelling distraction.* If what you are shooting for is worth your undivided attention, it is a guarantee that there will be distractions, toxic people, and voices in your head, all attempting to divert you. The only way to success is to *say no to anything that would divert you from your goals and dreams.* Learn the skill of saying *no* to these forces and yes to the dream that God has put within your heart. If he planted the seed within you, he will bring it to pass:

> Declaring the end from the beginning
> And from ancient times things which have not been done,
> Saying, 'My purpose will be established,
> And I will accomplish all My good pleasure." (Isaiah 46:10 NASB)

You Can Deal with Failure

7

Learning starts with failure; the first failure
is the beginning of education.
—JOHN HERSEY

L et me ask you to take a moment and do some honest reflection. Find a quiet space where you can think without distraction and answer these questions:

When you have failed, what did you do as a result?

Did you feel bad about yourself?

Did you withdraw from the pursuit of whatever it was that you failed at?

Are you now doing the thing you failed at then?

Are you doing it successfully?

Is there anything you would like to do now that you are not doing because you might fail?

How you answer those questions, or more accurately, how you have lived out the answers to those questions, has the power to determine where you end up in life. Your answers will determine your success in the areas that you care about most. In this chapter we will explore the positive ways you can deal with inevitable failures on your path to your goals.

SAME STORY, DIFFERENT ENDINGS

One day at a seminar, I talked with a woman who was despairing over her dating life. She had withdrawn from the dating scene after a few rejections, and she now had virtually no hope of ever finding a relationship.

At the start of the year she had been determined to improve her somewhat nonexistent dating life. She had set some great goals to get things moving. She even surrounded herself with a support group and joined a dating service to meet new people. She got a couple of "matches" and went out with the guys. She had a decent time and was looking forward to a second date with both of them. But the calls never came. The men did not want to go out on second dates with her. Both of them had "moved on."

The woman was devastated. She withdrew from her supportive friends and stopped checking her e-mail for activity on the dating site. She turned into something of an MIA in the dating world. But worse than that, she felt awful.

When I asked her what was going on inside, she said things like, "I am such a loser. No one will ever want me. I don't know why I even tried. This is never going to work, I will always be alone."

I did not have much time to talk with her, but none of my encouragement or suggestions seemed to help. Her mind was made up. From her point of view it was hopeless and would never be any different.

Fast forward to a week later. I was talking to another woman who also committed herself to reviving a stagnant dating life. She, too, had set some goals and joined a dating service.

At first nothing happened. She got no responses. But instead of seeing herself as a loser, she asked herself, "I wonder what is wrong with the way I am doing this?" She called a friend who had been successful with online dating and got her to help rewrite her profile.

Soon the matches began to happen. She liked two of the men she dated and wrote back to them saying she had had a great time and would love to see them again. But nothing happened. Apparently neither of the men desired to see her again.

"Bummer," she said. But she continued her pursuit of dating.

Then another guy appeared on the scene, and they went out one evening. She liked him, and he called again. And again and again and again. She was having a good time and beginning to like this man quite a lot. So far, so good. Until . . . she got an e-mail saying, in effect, "It has been great hanging out with you, but I don't see a future for us. Hope this finds you well, and good luck."

Here she thought things were going well and instead she was faced with the classic let's-be-friends situation. Stunned and bewildered, the poor woman went into a little mini-shock. She was quite sad for a while and cried a bit with her friends. But then she regrouped and came to me for help.

She explained her feelings. "Well, that experience was tough. I really liked that guy. I thought things were really beginning to click with us, and I still don't know what went wrong." As she and I unpacked it together, we uncovered one of the problems. Her desperateness had caused her to become something of a people pleaser with him. In trying so hard to get him to like her, she had become less herself and, as a result, less interesting. Predictably, he lost interest and moved on.

However, she learned from that insight, and the next time she did it differently. She relaxed and became more herself. As a result, she found greater freedom in her dating. She was no longer bound by her concern about whether the man was interested, but instead allowed herself to be authentically who she was in the dating process. That was a big growth step for her.

Then it happened. She called me one day and said, "I think I have found him." And you know what? She was right. They married a year later.

Coincidentally, that same week I ran into the first woman again. "How is your dating life going?" I asked, thinking that by now she might have turned it around.

I could tell instantly that this was not the case. Her eyes began to water, and her chin began to quiver. "Not too good," she said. "Not too good."

I empathized with her and asked if she wanted to talk about it. She did, and I heard a very sad story. She had not been on any dates since that rejection of more than a year ago. She still felt that she was a loser, and no one would ever want her.

I reflected back to the last time we had talked and what had occurred. Then it hit me. She and the second woman had the exact same story—up to a point. Both had experienced a season of nothing good happening. Both had committed to changing that. Both had gotten active and stepped out into the game. Both had received some initial responses, and both went on a couple of dates. But that is where the similarities ended. *From there one went into despair and took a thousand steps backward, and the other moved on toward reaching her goal.* Same story, very different outcomes. What was the difference?

Was one woman more interesting? More attractive? More appealing in some way? Is that why one reached her goal while the other one didn't? Not at all. The outcomes were determined by the way these women answered the questions we listed at the beginning of this chapter. Look at how the two answered these questions and you will see that they responded to failure in very different ways.

Q: When you failed, what did you do as a result?

A: One withdrew and quit, and the other learned from her failure and kept going.

Q: Did you feel bad about yourself?

A: One saw herself as a loser, and the other didn't.

Q: Did you withdraw from the pursuit of whatever it was that you failed at?

A: One did, and the other didn't.

Q: Are you now doing the thing you failed at then?

A: One isn't, and the other is happy in a relationship.

Q: Are you doing it successfully?

A: One isn't, and the other is.

Q: Is there anything you would like to do now that you are not doing because you might fail?

A: One would like to be dating or in a relationship. The other doesn't have to worry about that anymore and has moved on to other goals.

These two women did the exact same things, up to a point: the point of failure. And from there, one went on to success and the other didn't. How to respond to failure is one of the most important lessons you can learn in life. And that is the lesson of this chapter.

SOME THINGS IN LIFE ARE CERTAIN, OR THE NATURE OF EVERYTHING

We have all heard it said that two things in life are certain: death and taxes. While that is true, there is also another certainty: failure. It is absolutely a given. It is the nature of everything. In fact, without failure we never succeed.

Think of the things that you do well. You probably walk okay, for example. And when you eat, you probably get most of your food in your mouth. But that was not always so, was it? If we had the video of your life, we would see you as a toddler going through walking and eating processes that look very little like your current level of performance. A lot of your steps would have ended with you on your face. A lot of your pasta would also have ended up on your cheeks and chin. If today you still walk and eat like you did then, second dates are likely to be rarities for you. But walking and eating do not present problems in your dating life today. The reason? You have gotten failure in those areas out of your system. You have done something called "learning."

The process went like this: you tried, and you didn't get it right. You walked three or four steps, then sat down hard on your padded area. You had a bad outcome. Your parents told you, "No problem. Try again." You tried again and got a little closer to the goal before you hit the carpet. Your parents helped you up and you walked ten feet this time—all the way to the couch. Your parents cheered. You made similar progress on the eating front. After many noodles falling to the table, the floor, and down your shirt, you finally got most of the pasta inside your mouth and managed to keep it there. Your parents clapped and said, "Way to go!" Before long those awkward tasks became second nature. You walked and ate without conscious effort and no one made a big deal of it. In fact, you got to the point where you were performing those tasks so well that your parents were even trying to curb them: "Don't eat that candy before dinner, and don't leave the yard." Success brings its own set of problems.

The point is that whatever is now second nature to you was at one time a very, very, daunting task, and you failed the first times that you tried it.

Failing at those tasks did not mean anything to you other than "try again." Failure brought no personal interpretation as to your lovability or capability or feelings about yourself or the world at large. Failure meant simply that the task was yet to be learned. Everything you now do as second nature has gone through that process. You did not do it well the first time, and yet you did it again and again until you figured it out. That is the nature of life. We try, we don't get it right, and we try again until we do. Then when the task is learned, we forget about the process of it and just do it, enjoying the result of the ability we have finally mastered.

There are people who date for fun, for example. They don't think once about rejection or the date not working out well. They just do it and enjoy it. The reason is that they have learned how, and now it is second nature. The jitters of adolescence, the shyness, and the misgivings are all in the past. They have become seasoned veterans.

In fact, the second woman, the one who learned to date well and ended up married, told me, "The change came when I began to be unaffected by rejection. I had always let rejection do me in. But the more I got with the program, the less it bothered me because I knew I was on a path, and one rejection was merely a step to the next step. Rejection actually became kind of funny sometimes."

The same thing goes for people who are successful at public speaking, making sales calls, playing championship golf matches, starting new businesses, interviewing for a new job, or whatever. They have gone through the failing part and now know how to do their job. *But they did not skip the failure part.* Their stumbles and falls are certainly on the video. But more often than not, the ones who are not doing well are stuck because they have not moved successfully through the failure cycle. They got hung up there.

The difference between the winners and those who are not winning is not that the winners do not fail.

They both fail, but the winners see it as normal, move through it well, and get past it. The others get stuck, not because they are incapable of doing whatever it is they are attempting, but because they are incapable of handling failure.

Lesson number one about failure is this: *whatever you wish to do, you will fail at it in the beginning.* Accept that reality. That is the nature of the world. Everything works that way. Of course you can always point to exceptions, like the person who hits a home run his first time at bat, or some other lottery winner. But those are the *exceptions* that prove the rule. Ninety-nine out of a hundred winners will tell you that failure was the way to success.

Let's look at nine steps you can take toward full ownership of your life, beginning with failure.

Step One: Normalize and Deal with Failure

To take ownership of your life and get to where you want to be, you must *take ownership of your failure.* To own it means to put your arms around it, take it home and claim it as yours, nurse it, feed it, and take care of it. It's like buying a car or a house. You are no longer leasing; it is *all yours,* and no one else is responsible for it. The good part of that is this: since you now own your life, you can add value to it, make improvements, control it, and ultimately reap the benefits of it. If you are not an owner, all you can do is complain to the landlord, which, as we have seen, is what a lot of people do with their lives. They act as if someone else owns their life and they are renters. So when things don't go right, they just complain. The problem is that they have to live in their life, so it makes good sense to own failure so they can fix it up.

The first step, then, is to normalize failure. Accept the reality that it is a normal part of life. Do that and you won't get knocked off your horse when something doesn't work out. It won't surprise you. You will accept it, take God's hand, and go solve that problem. If you have trouble getting in touch with the reality of inevitable trouble, remember the words of Jesus: "In this world you will have trouble. But take heart! I have overcome the world" (John 16:33 NIV). Expect trouble and failure, but also expect that taking courage and joining him to work it out will get you over the hump and to your goal.

Why doesn't everyone who encounters failure pick himself up and try again? Why does one woman get rejected on a couple of dates then go on to find the love of her life, while another who gets rejected, quits? Why does one person make a sales call, get rejected, and later that month land the big account, while another gives up? The answer: one has normalized failure and learned how to deal with it, while the other has not. Let's look at why and how.

Step Two: Find Out What Failing Means to You

Now that you have accepted the fact that failure is normal in the process of becoming successful, you are ready for the next step. But before you take that step, let's prepare the way by exploring a few questions to check your present thinking on what happens when you fail.

What do you feel when you fail? (In other words, when you are rejected for a date or do not close the deal or your venture goes belly up.)

Do you feel bad and get deflated? (Not mere disappointment, but a judgment about yourself that plunges you into immobilizing emotional states.)

Does all hope go out of you? (A feeling that things will never be any different.)

Do you tell yourself that you are a loser? (Internal dialogue leads you to pin a global, critical label on yourself.)

Do you think that success is for others and not you? (You feel you are missing something that others have.)

Do you think that there is just no answer for your dilemma? (It's beyond anything you can learn or grow into, no matter how hard you try.)

Do you feel guilty? (A gnawing feeling that you should have been able to do this.)

Do you feel like it is all your fault? (An accusing, shaming, condemning feeling.)

Do you go into the "all bad" position? (Losing sight of your abilities, strengths, talents, aptitudes.)

Do you begin to hate God and think that he is not for you? (The feeling that God has let you down, or even has it in for you.)

Many people respond to failure in these ways because *they interpret the failure to have a specific, harmful meaning.* But as we have shown above, this is the wrong way to look at failure. The accurate meaning of failure is that it is a learning experience—a time to learn about ourselves, to learn the skills needed to master an endeavor we want to accomplish, or to learn more about the nature of the endeavor itself. But instead of seeing it as time to learn, many interpret failure in other ways that set them up to stop trying, as the list above shows. Usually, those negative interpretations come from our previous experiences. Failure has taken on bad meanings acquired from painful experiences in our families growing up or in other significant relationships.

The meanings that failure has for us come from our past experiences and relationships. They affect us in several significant categories: our view of ourselves, our view of others, our view of the world and how it works, and our view of God. When we go into new situations, we experience them through those grids, belief systems, emotional reactions and patterns of behavior that we have built through past experiences of failure or difficulty.

For example, if my experiences have made me feel like a loser, then I take that belief into new situations. If I fail in a new endeavor, I experience that new failure as confirmation of my negative belief about myself. "See, I knew it. I *am* a loser. I will never be able to make anything work. I'm just not capable." Or, we might have a bad experience with a person, and it means to us that "people will always hurt me or let me down." Or, "God is against me," or "The world itself is just too hard to figure out. There is no real way to make things turn out well."

These meanings become part of our makeup, and they live in our hearts, minds, and souls. They operate immediately and subconsciously, without our awareness that we are even following them. They cause us to live out patterns of behavior and choices that correspond to those particular meanings. We react defensively, protectively, aggressively, or withdraw from the game and quit trying. This happens because our life experiences have infused these meanings for failure into our character, and when we fail, they automatically kick in and take over. We lose our ability to choose and respond.

Look at your history of trying things in the areas where you feel stuck. Look at the areas that most depress you and in which you have stopped trying. Those are the places where it is most likely that you are operating by old messages and experiences. Figure out what those are. Listen to your thoughts and the voices in your head. Observe your feelings about those areas. You will learn the reason why you have given up or feel so negative about trying again. When you recognize where these old messages come from, you can reject them and break free of them. You can get support and validation from people on your team and rework the way you think and feel. But if you treat these old false messages as reality, then they will become reality. "I can't ever win" becomes a self-fulfilling prophecy.

Step Three: Go Ahead and Say It: "I Failed"

The first step to moving past failure is to call it what it is. But all too often those negative meanings we apply to failure shame us so much that we become afraid even to look at failure as reality. We become afraid even to say it:

"I failed."

"It didn't work."

"I blew it."

"Oh my gosh . . . did I ever not know what I was doing!"

"I screwed it up."

"I didn't have a clue to what I was doing. Have I ever got a lot to learn!"

What is so hard about that? It is actually empowering and freeing not to have to hide from failure, but to embrace it and admit it. Watch the people who do. Check out the winners who laugh about their failures. They are relaxed and comfortable because they have gotten out of the image protection business. And, they are so endearing. The people who own and talk about their mistakes as *their* mistakes are much more connectable and easy to identify with. They are not hung up in the useless business of trying to impress themselves or others. Instead, they are into results. People like this are so refreshing, and the good news is that you can be one of them.

Get around people who are honest about their shortcomings. They are infectious. You will like them, and they will help you become more comfortable about facing yours. Enter the land of freedom . . . where you can admit imperfection. It is a wonderful place to be, and others will respect and like you for being there.

Recently, our Web hosting company had a hardware meltdown. It was awful. For a good while we had no Web service or e-mail. When it first happened, we were bummed but not dismayed, because we got the word that we would only be down for a day. But the next day the news was worse. Their servers and backup servers had all crashed, and now the word came that repair was going to take longer. Since we work with publishers and organizations all over the country, to not have e-mail essentially means that we are shut down and cannot function. At that point things went from bad to really bad, as groups and media outlets were trying to get responses from us about scheduled speaking engagements and other time sensitive issues. But there was not much we could do.

I called the head of the IT company that had set us up with this hosting company and asked, "Why are we with a company that could allow this to happen? Can't we find someone else?" He assured me that for the services we needed, this host company was the best in the business and that they had his total trust. He described the events causing the crash as the "perfect storm" and said that there was nothing reasonable that they could have done to prevent it. His message was to hang in there. I trusted him, but I was more than a little bugged with the hosting company.

Then it got worse. The hosting company had been telling us that all the data would be recovered when they were up and running. But the unthinkable happened: they called me and said that they had recovered everyone's data . . . except mine. Mine was gone. Lost forever. My schedule, my e-mail, my archived mail from every organization I work with, and on and on. Everything that lived on the server had vanished never to be seen again. I could not believe my ears.

Fortunately, I discovered that the full computer backup I make myself do weekly had kept it all. I ended up losing only a day and a half of mail between my last backup and the failure. We got up and running again, apologized to everyone who had been waiting on us, and continued on. But at that moment I had less than zero confidence in our hosting company. They had not only gone down, they had gone down for a week! And then on top of that, they had erased my life. I still wanted my IT company to find a new host company.

But then everything changed.

I got an e-mail from the president of the host company, a message he sent to all of their accounts. I won't take up space printing the letter, but here are the essential elements of it:

- We really blew it. We were not prepared for what happened. It was our mistake.

- We are deeply sorry for the disruption that it caused you.

- Thank you to all who called and expressed your frustration to us, telling us of the things we could have done better to serve you.

- We took copious notes throughout the entire process in order to learn from what happened.

- Here is what we learned that we should have done differently.

- Here is what we have done to fix the vulnerability and correct those mistakes.

- Here are the things that we learned that we did right.

- Here are the changes that we are making.

- Here are some suggestions for you to protect yourself as well.

- We understand if you want to switch companies, and if you do, we will be glad to help you and make the transition as painless as possible.

Immediately my whole attitude changed. I was dealing with a winner here, not a loser. I felt that as long as this guy was leading the company, I was in good hands. Why, because he never failed? *No.* It was because when he failed, he owned it, admitted it, and put his arms around it to learn from it. He used his failure as a step toward becoming a great company. That is what gave me confidence, not the fact that he had not made mistakes. Give me a person who makes a mistake and knows what to do with it anytime over someone who does not own his failures.

Can't you see another company excusing, blaming, and not owning its failure in a crisis like this? "It's not our fault! It's the power surges, the crummy hardware providers, the complicated nature of Windows. Call your manufacturer or your software provider, this is not our problem." Excuses like these are the first line of defense on most technical help lines. "Someone else is responsible, not us. It's not our fault."

But here was a winner. I immediately wrote the president of that company a letter and thanked him for his ownership and leadership. I told him that was why our company would be sticking with him.

I urge you to join the winners who own their failures and learn from them. All the energy you consumed protecting yourself from failure or defending yourself when you failed or beating yourself up because you failed will be channeled into solving problems and learning from them.

Step Four: Learn from It

In the story of the Web hosting company, we can see what I like to call the "autopsy" of a failure experience. When something does not go right, don't beat yourself up or get on your case about it. *Use it to your advantage!* You spent a lot of good energy, and probably money, time, resources, relationship equity, and other assets on this lesson. So wring everything out of it that you can. Figure out such things as:

- What you did wrong

- What you did right

- What you missed along the way

- What choices you made that you don't want to make again

- Why you made them and what weaknesses contributed to those mistakes

- What support would have helped you

- What new skills you need to develop to make it different the next time

- What teachers or mentors or counselors or consultants you might want with you

- What about this situation reveals a pattern that you have seen before

- What blind spots you have about yourself or others that led to this

In my speaking and counseling on marriage, dating, and relationships, I see one theme over and over. Some people who experience a failed relationship repeat the same failure with every new relationship they find. They do not learn. They just keep on going without addressing the things that contributed to the last failure. Others, however, figure out their contribution to the problem, learn from it through divorce recovery or counseling, do the necessary work, and then move on to make better choices. They learn from each mistake so they do not have to make that one again.

We have seen that mistakes are normal. They are the progression of learning. Think back to the second grade and the mistakes you made as you learned to read or write or do math. What if you had just ignored those mistakes? What if your teacher had let you continue on down the path without correcting them? You would have made the same mistakes again, and you would have repeated that grade over and over. Then in real life you would face all sorts of problems, ranging from an inability to get a job to an inability to make your finances work. In other words, *until we learn to get it right, we will repeat the mistake.* If you learn from your mistake, however, you can correct it and move on to the next grade, the next level of relationship, or the next level of work.

Step Five: Get Forgiveness

There is an immutable law in the universe that comes right out of the Bible: whatever is under judgment does not improve. It gets worse. In other words, as long as you feel guilty and condemned for your failure, it will not get better. It will stay the same, at best, or it will get worse. It is under the law of condemnation. You will not get better by feeling guilty, mad at yourself, ashamed, afraid, or any of those negative emotions. You will get better only by finding grace, or "unmerited favor" from God and other people. As you are accepted "in your failure," the sting and the power of condemnation will go away, and you will be free to look at the problem instead of your guilt and fear.

To illustrate, let's say a child makes a mistake on her math homework. When her dad sees the mistake, he begins to berate her, put her down, and make her feel guilty. What do you think she is focused on at that moment? Learning math? I don't think so. Her entire being is focused on how bad she is, what a loser she is, how afraid of her father she is, or how mad at him she is, what a jerk he is, how she hates school, how she wants to run away, and on and on. Whatever is going through her head, it is not about getting better at school. The wrath and condemnation have done one thing only: they have diverted the focus away from the real issue, which is the girl's math performance.

To improve in areas of failure, you must receive forgiveness and grace. You have to get with people and with God and understand the most liberating message of the entire world: if you want forgiveness, God gives it. He forgives you for anything you do. And good people will do the same. But to realize that forgiveness, you have to talk to these people. You have to open up to them, confess to them, and allow them to know you and love you in your failure.

Put down the fig leaf; take off the mask. Open up to some safe people about your failures, and show them the reality of who you are. When they accept you, you will learn to accept yourself as well. Then the sting of failure will go away and the freedom to get better will kick in. You will look like Tiger Woods on the practice tee, hitting a shot and watching it to see how it went. You won't find him standing there beating himself up and feeling guilty about a slice that sailed into the rough. He just corrects his swing to make the next shot better.

If you do not find forgiveness from outside of yourself, then you will not have it on the inside. It takes forgiveness from others to affirm our perception of our own value when we fail. Ask God, and he will grant it. But also show your failures to others who accept you and you will internalize their love.

If you have failed others, go to them and own your mistake and seek their forgiveness. If there is something more to be done, make amends. Make it right. In doing that, you will help those you have failed in the same way you failed them. You will also be restored to them, overcome your own guilt, and become an altogether different person than the one who failed them. In seeking forgiveness and making amends, you become a healing agent to the one you hurt, and that is a huge improvement, not only for you, but also for the relationship and for the person you failed. God sees forgiveness and making amends as so important that he tells us to get right with others before we try to approach him: "First go and be reconciled to your brother; then come and offer your gift" (Matthew 5:24 NIV).

Step Six: Look at Your Responses

We have seen how important it is to look at the meaning that you attribute to failure, because negative feelings and conclusions can cause you to remain stuck. The next step is to figure out what you do at that point. In order to do that, you must evaluate those feelings and conclusions. How did they affect your responses to failure, and what can you do differently?

When you fail, do you:

- Withdraw?

- Get angry at yourself?

- Get angry at someone else?

- Give up?

- Not try again?

- Change courses impulsively?

- Eat, drink, or medicate yourself in some unhealthy way?

- Look for meaningless distractions that get you no closer to what you want?

- Make excuses?

- Blame?

- Avoid looking at it and remain in denial?

- Run to some area of strength to make yourself feel better instead of looking at your weakness?

The negative meanings you place on failure and your emotional reactions to it always generate accompanying behavioral patterns. You must uncover your own negative patterns and take steps to change them. To do that, you will probably need some support from outside yourself—a group, an accountability partner, a counselor, or some outside structure. Old patterns usually do not change as a result of willpower or just by making different commitments. Such changes require outside support.

An addict's life changes when he realizes that his pattern of response to failure is to return to the drug. To change this failure pattern he must attend a meeting to find the support he needs to resist returning to the drug. He has to interrupt his predictable pattern of response to failure. Going to the meeting instead of using the drug changes the pattern. To change your own patterns, you must have that same kind of structure waiting in the wings of your life—a structure you can turn to for support when you fail to overcome those patterns in the aforementioned list.

The most important tip we can give you in pursuing any goal may be to ask these questions: What will I do when the failure pattern hits me the next time? Who will I call, or where will I go? What will I do differently?

When you find the answers to these questions, your chances of success will shoot way up.

Step Seven: Go for It Again

In one of my relationship seminars, a young man told me that the fear of rejection kept him from asking women out. "I can't handle rejection," he said. "How can I avoid it?"

My answer surprised him. I told him that he needed to get his rejection numbers up, not down. "I want you getting rejected a million times," I said. "Because if you are getting rejected that many times, it means that you are out there pursuing. And with that many attempts, some good things are sure to happen as well."

Remember, if failure is part of the process, then the more we fail, the more we are engaged in the process, and the more success we will find.

Persistence after failure is a huge key to success. The chapter coming up is on perseverance and persistence, so I won't address that subject in detail here. But we must include persistence in our thinking about failure, because failure is exactly when persistence is needed. We don't need it when we succeed; we need it on the path to success when we have not yet gotten there. In looking at failure, we always need to remember that to reach the goal will require many, many efforts.

Step Eight: Have the Funeral

In spite of the positive aspects of failure, we must be realistic and face the fact that in some cases failure is not merely a step in the accomplishment of a goal. It is a finality. The game is over. The company is bankrupt. The relationship has ended. There is no next step to be taken to make it work, because it is not going to work. It is the end of the road.

Winners know that and accept it. They embrace the failure and go through the grief process. They express their feelings about it, get angry and sad, grieve it, and move on. They do not do the useless things that keep people stuck, like chasing something dead that should be given up or sitting there protesting the reality of what is inevitable or has already occurred. Remember the example of the woman who had for thirty years remained bitter over the loss of her relationship. She should have had the funeral and moved on.

Solomon put it this way:

It is better to go to a house of mourning than to go to a house of feasting, for death is the destiny of every man; the living should take this to heart.

Sorrow is better than laughter, because a sad face is good for the heart.

The heart of the wise is in the house of mourning, but the heart of fools is in the house of pleasure. (Ecclesiastes 7:2–4 NIV)

When your goal is alive and has a chance of succeeding, the right thing to do is persevere. But when it is over, the right thing to do is to "go into a house of mourning." Sorrow, Solomon says, can be good for the heart. Mourning enables you to work through the loss, and then your heart will be available for new things. But if you don't lay the loss to rest and mourn it, then the heart still holds to the dead dream and is not available to win the next time. The woman who had lost a cherished relationship at forty would not lay her loss to rest and mourn it. She clung to the useless ghost of a dead relationship and thus for thirty empty and bitter years was not available to a new one. As a result of her inability to grieve, this woman experienced a much bigger loss than the loss of a relationship. She could have lost a relationship but had a life. Instead, she lost a relationship and a life.

Look your failure or loss right in the eye, have the funeral, express your feelings, and kiss it goodbye. Remember what Jesus said about remembering Lot's wife. She could not let go of her old life, and therefore she turned to salt instead of achieving a new life.

When experiencing the death of a dream, remember that not everything is lost. If you have gone through the loss process wisely, you have gained something extremely valuable. You have gained experience, learning, character growth, and the tools you need to never have to go through that failure again. As God tells us, *he can bring good out of all things, and he can cause your worst failure to work for your good.* Even if all your hard effort ends in the failure of a cherished goal, it never ends in nothing if we respond in his way.[1]

I like to look at it this way:

A winner owns his failure, and God owns his shame.

When we let God forgive us, comfort us, and be with us in the sting of failure, then we can face it and own it in the way that ultimately helps us. God takes the shame of it by offering us unconditional forgiveness and acceptance. Then we can grieve, not as those who have no hope, but as those who do have hope because we know that God is with us.

Step Nine: Learn that You Can Learn

There is a big difference between a victim and a winner. Victims see things the way they are and think they will always be that way, because uncontrollable forces are acting upon them. But winners have a different attitude, especially about failure and trying something new to see if it works better. They know one of the most important things we can ever know: *they know that they can learn.*

If your hope lies in your abilities, then you are on precarious ground. For if your dream works out because you are able to accomplish it successfully, then all is well. But if you put everything you have into your dream and it does not turn out well, where is your hope then? You have come to the end of your ability, and there is nothing there but failure.

But if you have in your toolkit another instrument of hope—your ability to learn—then virtually nothing seems hopeless. If you can't accomplish your dream now, you can learn how to do it. Winners think this way every day, and it is not just some form of self-esteem jargon, it's something much deeper than that. It is hope in the very nature of the way God created the universe and our relationship to it. It is like having hope in gravity.

God made humans with the ability to learn in a more complex way than any other creature. We can observe what we need to know to accomplish a goal, and then we can pursue that knowledge. We can learn with a *purpose* in mind. He gave us the ability not only to achieve the purpose, but also the ability to actually do the learning required to achieve it. You *can* learn to do what you need to do:

- A couple can learn to communicate.

- A depressed person can learn to overcome depression.

- A parent with a child out of control can learn how to discipline effectively.

- A person without a career can learn a new skill.

- A person with a weight problem can learn how to lose weight and keep it off.

- A person without faith can learn about God.

- A person who gets a bad job review can learn to do better.

- A person with a pattern of failed relationships can learn the relationship skills that are needed.

- A person who picks bad people over and over can learn why that happens and how to spot the bad ones.

When you know that you can learn, you don't need to feel stuck. You see failure as a step in getting to the end point because it shows you that there is some kind of information or skills or wisdom or knowledge that you need to learn in order to get there. And because you believe that you can learn, you are not hopeless, but empowered.

Every week John and I do a public seminar called "Solutions." We have been doing it for years, and now it is available by satellite broadcast across the country, probably at a location near you.[2] Exposure to thousands of people in these seminars has given us the opportunity to hear one thing over and over again. It is the theme of a person moving from hopelessness to fulfillment through *learning God's ways to do life, and putting them into practice.* We continually hear people say things like, "I had no hope when I first came here, and now everything is different."

What is different? Did the world change? No, it is the same. What changed is this: they found the truth of Proverbs to be real when it says, "Know also that wisdom is sweet to your soul; if you find it, there is a future hope for you, and your hope will not be cut off" (Proverbs 24:14 NIV). *Listen to that!* It says to *know* this powerful source of hope: *wisdom.* Wisdom leads to hope.

If you believe that finding the wisdom needed for a certain situation will reveal an answer, then you will always have hope in the power of learning. It is a lesson that will serve you for the rest of your life.

ONLY THE BEST FAIL

We often see people who remain in a stable job for ten, twenty, or thirty years. They may call their job a career, but it isn't really. Instead of experiencing newness and growth in each of those years, they relive the same year ten, twenty, or thirty times. In their thirtieth year they are no different from the way they were in their first year. They are not trying anything new, and they are not growing. It is the same old same old. Often they remain in stagnation and never step out of the rut because of a fear of failure. As a result, they never become the best at anything, or what is worse, they never achieve their own "personal best." They refuse to fail, and only those who fail become the best.

Those who will not risk failure are very different from the others in stable jobs who have grown each year and learned along the way. Their thirty years on the job are all different years, not the same year repeated over and over.

What would you do if your goal was a political career and the following things happened to you? The love of your life dies; you have a nervous breakdown; you fail as a businessman; you are defeated when you run for state legislator; you lose a job; you are defeated when you run for speaker of the state house; you are defeated for nomination to Congress; you lose a re-nomination; you are rejected to become a land officer; you are defeated for the U.S. Senate; you are defeated for the nomination of vice president; you are again defeated for the Senate.

How would you feel? Would you withdraw from the race? Would you think you are a loser? Would you think you are nuts to believe you could ever accomplish anything in politics? Would you give up? Or, would you become president of the United States and one of most heralded leaders of all time, negotiating one of our country's most difficult periods of history and literally saving the country as we know it today? If you could handle failure, you would do exactly that. You would be Abraham Lincoln.

Lincoln knew the truth of the Bible, which says, "For though a righteous man falls seven times, he rises again, but the wicked are brought down by calamity" (Proverbs 24:16 NIV). With faith and the understanding that failure is not the end but common to all good people, you, too, can get up and rise to the heights that God desires for you. Who knows, you might even become president!

8

You Can Persist and Persevere

8

Sure I am of this, that you have only to endure to conquer.

—WINSTON CHURCHILL

If you are like millions of people around the world, at some point in your life you have driven or ridden in a Honda car or motorcycle. Ever wonder how those vehicles came into being? Did a guy named Honda sit down one day, design an automobile, run out and sell it to your local dealer, who in turn sold it to you? It was not quite like that.

In the late 1930s, Soichiro Honda built a little workshop while still in school. He was developing the concept of the piston ring and wanted to sell the idea to Toyota. He worked on his design so long he often slept in the workshop. Married now, he would not give up on his idea, even though he had to pawn his wife's jewelry for working capital.

But when he finally presented a working sample to Toyota, the engineers laughed at his design. Nevertheless, Honda did not give up. Rather than focus on his failure, he returned to school and kdept redesigning. Two years later he won a contract with Toyota.

Now he needed a factory. Unfortunately, the government was preparing for war and Honda couldn't find building supplies. Instead of quitting, he invented a new concrete-making process that enabled him to build the factory.

Then the factory was bombed twice.

Did that stop Honda? No. He collected what he called "gifts from President Truman"—surplus gasoline cans discarded by American fighters—which became his new raw materials for his rebuilt manufacturing process.

Then an earthquake destroyed the factory.

Was Honda finally defeated? Postwar Japan was experiencing an extreme gasoline shortage that forced the Japanese people to walk or ride bicycles. The persistent inventor applied his creativity to his own situation and built a tiny engine for his bicycle. His neighbors saw it and wanted one too, but he had no materials with which to build copies.

However, having survived rejection, ridicule, shortages, war, and natural disasters, Soichiro Honda was not ready to give up. He sent an inspiring letter to 18,000 bicycle shop owners, requesting donations toward a new idea that might help him revitalize Japan. Money came in from five thousand people and Honda set forth to build tiny bicycle engines. After trial and error he produced the small engine Super Cub, which was a huge success in Japan. Honda's company took off and he began to expand to European and American markets.

Honda didn't stop responding to the realities of the market. Noting a severe gas shortage in the United States in the 1970s and a growing interest in small cars, Honda's company began developing vehicles smaller than anyone had seen before and changed the automotive industry forever. Today the Honda Company, with more than 100,000 people in Japan and in the U.S., is one of the largest automobile companies in the world. All because one determined inventor committed himself to an idea, acted on it, adjusted when he needed to, and never gave up. Failure was simply not considered a possibility.[1]

An amazing story, isn't it? Few people who get into their Hondas have any idea what it took to put that car in their driveway. But the truth is that most things of great value in life are achieved in exactly the same way, *especially the things that not everyone accomplishes.* Those things that most everyone does don't take a lot of perseverance, and therefore, most everyone does them. The more value something has, the more perseverance it takes to get it.

For example, most people can find lunch. Especially in America. Even if the one restaurant is closed, it's no big deal to find another one down the street. Normal day-to-day things like that seldom take a lot of persistence. Even people with little drive or with dissatisfied lives accomplish them. But persistence is almost always a big component to accomplishing the things of real value. I'm referring to things such as:

- Reaching a business or financial goal

- Reaching a personal goal like losing a significant amount of weight

- Mastering a skill

- Having a good marriage

- Raising well-adjusted kids

- Building a successful career

- Starting a business

- Overcoming depression

- Building a community of friends

- Developing an employee or team of people

- Getting in shape

- Overcoming an illness or living with one

- Working out a difficult marriage

- Making dating work successfully

- Overcoming an addiction

- Overcoming an emotional problem or habit pattern

Think about the people you know who have accomplished any of the above. In the vast majority of those cases, you will see one thing to be true: *they accomplished their goal through persistence.* No one who accomplishes the hard things does it quickly or easily. It comes about through continued effort. As Mr. Honda said, "To me success can be achieved only through repeated failure and introspection. In fact, my success represents the one percent of the work that resulted from the ninety-nine percent that was called failure."

In the chapter on failure we saw the importance of looking at failure in just that way. But that is only the first step. In this chapter, we will see what is required as the next step: continuing on through persistence and perseverance.

NOTHING HAPPENS OVERNIGHT OR WITHOUT A FIGHT

My three-year-old daughter often wants things, as we all do. But I notice something in her that concerns me for her future. She wants hers *now*. And she wants them without having to do anything for them. Not only does she not want to wait for dessert, she does not want to have to eat her green beans to get the cookie. Imagine that. She is not bad; she's just three. She is what we refer to as "childish." That means lacking the maturity necessary to realize that you can't have everything when you want it, nor can you have it without giving something first. What's worse, she has no interest in developing those abilities. Therefore, they have to be built in from the outside by a process called discipline.

As her father, that process is what I must focus on—giving her the gifts of persistence and perseverance. If I can give her those two things, she will end up with the cookies of life, the rewards that will be what the Bible calls "sweet to her soul," as she "accomplishes the desires of her heart" in the future.[2] To get what she wants in life, my daughter must first possess these two important qualities. So I have to persist and persevere in the process of instilling them into her.

When we see this kind of immaturity in a small child, we think nothing of it because we expect it. We laugh at the sweetness of the immaturity that wants the cookies of life now and without effort. Little children think, "the world should exist to make me happy." And when it doesn't make them happy, they cry "foul," as if something is wrong. In limited doses and at very young ages, this is cute to watch. But too much of any good thing can make you sick, and that is why every parent eventually reaches the boiling point when faced with the demand for instant gratification and the protest when it is not forthcoming. We understand the desire in small children, but as they grow we expect them to develop a more mature attitude toward their desires and realize that the world does not owe them instant gratification. Things worth having require effort, persistence, and perseverance.

All too often, though, even adults hang on to the childish desire for instant gratification. It is seldom as obvious in adults as it is in children, especially when it operates within ourselves. You think you're not guilty? Well, maybe not, but before you make that claim, consider whether you've been affected by any of these examples of "I want it now, and I want it without difficulty."

- Quick weight-loss plans and diets that promise easy reduction of pounds with little effort

- Quick money-making plans, infomercials, or strategies that always emphasize how "fast" and "easy" it will be to have your mansion or your yacht

- Buying lottery tickets in hopes of winning it all

- Following hasty romantic passion and thinking it will result in a meaningful, lasting relationship

- Thinking that a career rise or job promotion should just come to you because you "deserve it" or have talent

- The desire for a quick or short-term therapy to resolve deep-seated emotional and relational issues

- Thinking that a little "quality time" with a child will be all the parenting needed for his or her development

- A mountaintop experience equaling spiritual maturity and intimacy with God

Can't most of us admit that at one time or another we have gotten hooked into one of these strategies? It is human nature to want the easy route, or the quick fix, or to get to the top without paying our dues, and almost everyone succumbs to this temptation at some point. But as reality imposes itself on us, we learn that to think that way is only a childish fantasy, a wish, and it will not yield any real rewards in the real world. Bummer.

But hang on. That feeling of being bummed out when the something-for-nothing attempt does not work is important, as my three-year-old is discovering. She still wants the cookie, and she is bummed because she doesn't have it. She has a father who is standing in the way of her getting it without doing the hard thing first.

When we put those two elements together—the desire for the cookie and the impossibility of getting it without doing the hard work first—we have the beginnings of the formula for getting what she wants. Her desire, added to the discomfort of being bummed out, alongside the requirement to finish her vegetables, causes her to do the thing required to get the prize: persevere through the requirement to the goal. As Proverbs says, "The laborer's appetite works for him; his hunger drives him on" (16:26 NIV). And when she gets that cookie, it is a joy to see her happy excitement.

People reap the rewards promised in the examples we just listed by the same process. Not through the "instant and easy" methods promised, but with the only formula that works: "later and effort." The words *later* and *effort* correspond to the two words that are the subject of this chapter: *persistence* and *perseverance*. These two words are quite similar to one another, but one of them adds a slightly different twist to the basic idea.

Persistence means that it will take steadfast effort in the face of difficulty to get there. Perseverance adds the element of delayed gratification. Persistence tells us it is hard work to begin with, and then perseverance tells us it gets even harder because we encounter difficulties that put the gratification even further out, and therefore we have to be steadfast in pushing through to the end. In other words, to achieve your goal you must *persist*: get at it and keep at it. And then you must *persevere*: keep at it even when the going gets tough.

"Oh, puleeeze!" we cry. "There has got to be a better way! Surely there is a shortcut." Well, yes, there usually is. There are quick paths to seeming rewards in most areas of life. But those rewards are only "seeming," as the results do not last.

- Weight-loss research shows that those who lose it quickly do not keep it off and even gain back more than they lost. Further, the later gain is tougher to lose than the first.

- The majority of lottery winners are bankrupt within a short time. The *majority* lose the millions that they won.

- Quick "falling in love" and coupling based only on romantic feelings without relationship skills to back them up ends in dissatisfaction and often a push to find another relationship on the rebound.

- Career advancement that comes from nepotism or favoritism or inheritance that is without merit blows up or fails in the end.

- Quick "feel good" therapies that do not involve character changes result in relapse.

- Intermittent "quality" parenting does not provide the ongoing molding of character that children require.

- Subjective mountaintop spiritual experiences fade and do not yield the kind of faith and maturity that ongoing spiritual disciplines bring about.

But even these failed attempts can bring about something good, just like it does with a three-year-old. If they cause you to realize the reality that "quick and easy" will not get you there, and you still have that strong, unrealized longing, then you have the two elements needed for success: motivation and a path.

You want it, and now you know how to get it: do the work, one step at a time, and realize that the reward will come at the end of the work. Applied to the list above, this means:

- Every day, people do lose weight and keep it off. Lots of it, as the research proves. The way they do it is with a little effort, time, and patience. They lose it slowly, not quickly, through structured, sustainable methods. They do not starve themselves or work out around the clock. They get into a healthy lifestyle and stay there on an ongoing basis. Therefore, they not only lose the weight, they keep it off. Why? Because they are now doing what every person does who stays in shape: eat healthy and exercise. There are no skinny people eating and living like the ones who are overweight, just as there are no rich people spending more than they have and running up debt on credit cards.

- Every day, people do achieve financial independence. But they do not do it quickly without effort. The effort is not back breaking, but it requires what we are talking about here. A little work and some delay of gratification. They let time do its compounding work. At the business level, they do it the same way, slowly, diligently, and with sustainable methods. Get any good financial planning book and you can see the formula for yourself.

- Every day, people do have good, lasting relationships. But they have them as a result of working on their communication, forgiveness, acceptance, character, intimacy, vulnerability, sacrifice for each other and the relationship, and delay of gratification when things get hard.

- Every day, people do hard work, increase their education and training, practice diligence, do jobs they do not like and are not their ultimate goal, take risks and stretch themselves, recover after failure, and so on, to build satisfying careers. They earn where they end up by doing the hard work to get there, as opposed to expecting it to be handed to them because they are "special."

- Every day, people do recover from emotional and relational problems, addictions, and other struggles. But they do it by consistently working on their patterns, delaying the instant relief that their addictions and defenses would afford them, and doing the hard work of learning to relate and handle things differently.

- Every day, people raise healthy kids who function well and are able to adapt to life. But they do it with consistent self-sacrifice that gives them the time and energy to pour massive amounts of love, structure, discipline, and coaching into their children on an ongoing basis.

- Every day, people do develop the kind of faith that is fulfilling, meaningful, exciting, and sustaining in the worst crises of life. But they do it through the practice of the time-tested, age-old spiritual disciplines and consistency.

Here is the big idea: you can get the results that you are looking for in various areas of life *if you do it the way that the people who get the results do it.* They do it through persistent effort and perseverance. That is the only way.

GETTING IT AND KEEPING IT REQUIRES MUSCLE

At a recent gathering I overheard a group of people talking about hurrying out to buy lottery tickets. The lottery that week had climbed to an astronomical figure, which had this little group beside themselves with excitement. I poked my head into the circle and asked, "So, why do you want to go bankrupt?"

They looked at me as if I were from another planet, and then one of them said, "We aren't talking about going bankrupt. We are talking about winning millions!"

"Yeah, I know," I said. "But the majority of the people who win go bankrupt. So it looks to me like that is what you are signing up for."

They looked at me a little strangely, as if I were dousing their dream with a bucket of cold water. I don't think they believed me. Even if they did, no doubt they were convinced that they would be among the few who actually held on to their winnings. We did not have time to get into the reason that most lottery winners become losers, but if we had, I would have told them that there is a good reason.

It is the same reason that people who lose weight quickly or fall in love impulsively soon end up back where they started. It happens because they did not build the result, and therefore they do not have the skills to maintain the result. The same skills that create a result are needed to hold on to it and make it work.

Maintaining a good weight requires self-control and a healthy lifestyle. If a person doesn't have those two things, weight gain is a sure thing, period. On the other hand, if they develop those two required elements, and through persistence lose the weight, they will have the skills needed to keep it off. But if they don't, they won't.

If a person builds financial independence through delay of gratification, impulse control, and good self-management, then when he gets it, he will be able to keep it. But give an impulsive person a lot of sudden money and, as the old saying goes, "a fool and his money are soon divided." Following one path causes you to lose in two ways, while following the other causes you to win in two ways. In the quick and easy way you lose first because that way doesn't work, and then you lose again because you do not become the kind of person who can ever sustain the process and make it work. In the reality way, the way of diligence and persistence that God designed, you win because you are doing things in the way that actually brings results, and then you win again because you are becoming the kind of person who can keep your success after you achieve it.

As we have seen, delay of gratification is a big part of this path. Research has shown, for example, that delay of gratification is a better predictor of children's future success than IQ or SAT scores. When it comes to achievement, brains and talent or good-luck windfalls do not seem to be nearly as important as good character. There is just something about having to do things in the "old-fashioned" way that always brings people out on top. *Do the work first; play later.*

In the process of persistence, character is built. Muscle is developed. Maturity is gained. As James tells us, "Consider it pure joy, my brothers, whenever you face trials of many kinds, because you know that the testing of your faith develops perseverance. Perseverance must finish its work so that you may be mature and complete, not lacking anything" (1:2–4 NIV).

The same principle says you have to allow a little birdie to break out of its own shell instead of breaking the shell for it and bringing it out before its time. Part of it is the timing involved in maturity, but another part is the actual persistent process of the bird's having to peck the shell and work its way out. That process builds strength and muscles that it will need to survive in the outside world. Break the bird out yourself and it will die because it is not ready to handle life. It did not get there the "old-fashioned" way of delaying gratification and earning its reward of freedom. So it dies, too weak to make it in the real world.

But this slower, surer process is so against our nature. We want it *now*, and so we focus on getting the goal but not gaining the skills. The other night I was working with my other daughter, who is six, on her reading. She has figured out that recognizing words is the quick and easy way, and that phonics takes a bit of work. She loves it when she sees words she already knows and can just skip along the page and read them. It is exciting for her to go through a whole sentence without hitting a speed bump. She loves the prize, being able to read.

She was reading a book to me and was breezing along when she hit a pretty big word that she was not familiar with. She stumbled a little bit and then tried to skip ahead, regaining that feeling of momentum. But I had to rain on her parade. "Wait. Go back Speedy. What is that word?" I asked.

"I don't know. It's too hard," she said.

"That doesn't matter if you sound it out," I said. "If you sound out the letters, you can read any word you ever find. So come on. What are the sounds?"

I could see her having to go deep into the well and summon up the perseverance to get through four formidable syllables and some testy sounds. She had no clue what the word was or where these sounds were going to take her. I had to nudge her through each syllable, each consonant, each vowel.

As she painstakingly pushed through each sound, she could hear each of the previous ones still reverberating until finally she got to the end. She had said the word piece by piece without recognizing it, and then when she put it all together and said it at once, the light came on. She happily said it again and beamed with excitement. She was justifiably proud because she had done something that she didn't think she could do.

But what was important to me was not that she got the word. That was the fruit, the prize. I was delighted because she was learning the skill that would enable her to get *any* word. If she learned how to sound out the syllables, she would be able to read words that she did not know and had never seen before. Because she persisted in going through the work of it, she developed the muscle that James is talking about. In the area of reading, she was becoming "complete, lacking in nothing." *The big value of persistence and perseverance is in who we become as we persist and persevere.* We become the kind of people that we need to be if we are to make it.

Sometimes Obstacles Are Really Open Doors

The old saying, *God never closes a door without opening another one,* gives us one of the best reasons we have for perseverance. Life is a journey, and it usually involves going down a few dead ends before we get to where we are headed. We have seen that there is value in these unintended trips as we build our character and abilities along the way. But what we don't often realize is that the dead end, or the obstacle itself, might be a huge blessing in disguise. If we persist and persevere, we will find that one closed door turns us toward another opportunity, often a better one.

I once asked an audience how their lives would have been if they had gotten everything they thought they wanted. Groans and laughs erupted as they realized that they were much better off at having lost a certain relationship or opportunity than if it had worked out. What they thought they wanted was not what they needed. God knew better.

John and I (Henry) saw this truth brought to life in our own work about ten years ago. In the previous ten years, we had built a psychiatric hospital treatment company, and we loved the work we were doing. Every day was a joy and a new challenge. We were leading that company, doing the clinical work, developing treatment programs, writing the group materials for the hospitals to use, developing material on personal growth, and teaching in seminars throughout the western United States. In addition we did a syndicated radio show in the West and wrote books on our materials. It was all an outreach of the company, and it was the structure of the company that made it work and provided the needed resources. We found all of this extremely fulfilling.

Then, almost overnight, managed care and HMOs swallowed up the medical industry. Before this change, insurers had allowed patients to remain in a treatment center long enough to really work on their issues and bring about significant improvement. But with the new managed care models, they would no longer allow patients to stay in the hospital long enough to get real help. Patients could be in hospitals only long enough to get stabilized in acute or emergency situations. We were no longer able to do what we loved the most, to communicate and process the spiritual and psychological issues involved in a person's problem.

Suddenly the clinic turned into more of a business than a passion to help the hurting. Although the centers were still financially viable, we knew that it was no longer our calling. In addition, a merger had taken place that affected our company, and the new structure only increased the problem and moved us further away from our calling. We could not work with that, so we knew it was time to get out.

I recall those days, and they were dark, at least in the beginning. We had spent the better part of ten years and a lot of sacrifice and hard work building a company, and we were finally at the point where it was mature and doing well. We were enjoying the fruits of our dream. Then, wham! The gut punch. The door slammed in our face. All that we had poured into our dream went down the drain. "God, how could you let this happen?"

What we didn't know, or at least had forgotten and were too blind to see, was "where God closes one door, he opens another." In the getting-out phase, we sat down with the company we sold to and talked to see if there was some way we could work together. We had little hope of anything developing. All that we had built seemed to be going away, but we decided to persist and persevere in the process. If there was even a slim chance that we could find some way to use all that we had built, we wanted to find it. Then from the long meetings and back and forth communications, an idea emerged.

The new company had just acquired a broadcast that reached into two hundred markets around the country. Those clinical services that they were continuing needed an outreach, so they asked us to be the doctor experts on that call-in broadcast. The idea sounded interesting, but what would our "real job" be if we were no longer in the hospital treatment business?

Then it hit us. If we were talking daily to millions of people all across the country, we could start a company that took the things we were passionate about into communities. We had previously done this as a sideline in connection with our treatment centers; now we could do that in a more focused and larger way. So we started down a new path. We produced seminars for our listening audience and began helping churches and organizations use the materials that we developed to address life issues through small groups and other strategies. In addition to those primary broadcasts, we now have weekly satellite broadcasts in over three thousand churches, where audiences gather to hear our *Solutions* television broadcast and then go into small groups to work on their issues.

Now, years later, we have the privilege of working with thousands of churches and organizations through our materials and our speaking, partnering with them to do the amazing work of restoring lives, relationships, and dreams of people in their communities. Every day we receive letters and calls or talk to people in our travels who tell us of the life change they experienced through one of our groups, books, videos, or workbooks. This excites us, because people whom we've never met *have been touched through the work of other people using our materials.* The fruitfulness of our work has been multiplied, not by us, but by others.

We were bummed when our plan slammed in our face ten years ago. But God is bigger than our plans, and he always has a better one than any we could conceive ourselves.

As we went through this difficult time, I remember leaning on the verse that says, "Trust in the LORD with all your heart and lean not on your own understanding; in all your ways acknowledge him, and he will make your paths straight" (Proverbs 3:5–6 NIV). I did not understand why he had let us spend all that time and effort building something that would so soon cease to exist. It seemed like such a waste. I could not see at the time that it was not a waste at all. God was going to use all the material and models that we developed in a context much larger than our original plan—a context that would enable us to do much more good. Now, with the advantage of 20/20 hindsight, I confess that I can see what he was doing. I wish I had been more certain at the time that he knew what he was up to. I questioned him a lot, and I felt let down. But now I know what I should have known then: trust him. He is always up to something—something good.

If you have a relationship with God, this is true for you as well. Whenever you encounter a closed door, God knows what he is doing. Trust him; he is for you. He has a plan. But his plan will never come to fruition if you do not persist and persevere. That is your part, and making it all come together is his. If you stop when you encounter an obstacle or a closed door, you can't blame your failure on the obstacle or the door. If you stop trying at that point, then your ultimate failure is your own responsibility. Keep going until you find the right thing. The obstacle is there not to stop you, but to turn you toward a better way—God's way for your life. That's why persistence and perseverance are so vitally important. We have to press on, even when we hit obstacles and roadblocks. They might be the strengthening of the shell that we, like the birdie, have to break through in order to grow strong enough to succeed. Or they might be the closed doors that God uses to redirect our lives to his perfect plan. Really, now, in spite of the heartbreak and the agony of rejection, aren't you glad that the relationship you had in high school did not work out?

ONE STEP LEADS TO ANOTHER

The other big thing about persistence and perseverance is that the roadblocks themselves are often the steps that lead to the open door. One roadblock leads to another which leads to another which leads to success. If we quit at the first one, we don't find the lead that comes from the next one.

Think of it in terms of a salesman making calls. He knocks on one door and the purchasing agent does not want his product, but she remembers the name of a company that might. He calls on the buyer in that company and finds that he has no need for the product either, but he just heard someone at lunch talking about needing a product similar to what the salesman is selling. He gets the name and makes the call, and the voice on the line says, "I can't believe you are calling me. Your product is exactly what I have been looking for. When can you come by?"

You never know what might come from the next person you talk to or the next door you knock on. Remember, "for everyone who asks receives; he who seeks finds; and to him who knocks, the door will be opened" (Matthew 7:8 NIV). But if we quit asking, seeking, or knocking (read persisting and persevering), nothing can happen to fulfill that promise of an opened door.

Another way of looking at it is that each step always holds the step after it. The point of climbing a ladder or a flight of stairs is to get to the top. You don't make any given step your primary goal; you just see it as one more you must take to get to the top. But what if you focused on each step as if it had to be the top, getting angry or discouraged after your first step because you didn't immediately find yourself at the top? If that were your strategy, you would never get there. You take each step to get you to the next one.

Virtually everything works that way. We meet people who introduce us to other people who become the people we were looking for to begin with. We go to a doctor who figures out that we need another doctor and refers us to the right one. That is the way most of life works. People who stop and do not persist and persevere after the first steps don't work out are defying the way the system works, and they are sure to lose out on reaching their dream.

Here is another important thing to remember. Our explanations may make it seem that the persistence process leads you in a straight line, where one step always leads to the next one on a single linear path. That is not the way it works. Think of it not as a linear path, but as an innovative path. One step leads to an obstacle or a door that puts you on an entirely different path. It is not more of the same. But without the persistence of going through that step, we would not find the path that we eventually travel. Remember Mr. Honda and his piston rings? He ended up building the Accord and many other things bigger than just a ring on a piston in an automobile engine. But his persisting and persevering through the steps led to the innovation that led to the greater path.

What are you working on now that you need to follow through on to see where it leads? If you have met a dead end, it may mean that you need to take one more step—or two or three—before you find the path that leads to the reward you seek. The only thing that makes sense is to keep taking those steps. The open door is waiting for you on some path you are yet meant to find. If you don't find it because you fail to persist and persevere, it will be no one's fault but your own. God is for you. He wants you to win. And when you don't, he has something else for you that is part of his plan. So keep asking, seeking, and knocking, and you will find the door he has opened for you.

From Fruit Focus to Gardening Focus

Part of what we are talking about here is a change of focus. It is natural for us to look at the goal or the potential fruit of our hard work, and desire it. In fact, success research shows that to write down your goals, to have a vision for them, to keep them in mind, is very important to getting what you want in life. To be "goal oriented" is a wonderful thing. God has given us a linear mind that looks ahead to a desired result and then works out a path to achieve it. That is good.

But the ones who actually get there not only have a "goal orientation," they also have a "process focus." In other words, *to get to the goal they desire, they focus on the things that have to happen for it to come about.* That is the hard work of persistence and perseverance.

A wonderful analogy for this is the gardener, the farmer, or the vineyard keeper. Certainly these workers of the land want the eventual harvest, but just sitting around wanting is not what they do most of the year. What they do is work the fields. They sow the necessary seed, they water the plants, they dig around the root systems and purge them of things that choke them. They fertilize the plants to give them the ingredients that they can't produce for themselves. They prune them of the extraneous shoots and branches that distract their growth. They kill off diseases that may be infecting the plants, and they fight off insects and predators that come to steal what they are trying to produce. In other words, they can't be sitting around all year wishing or demanding that fruit come. Instead, they go to work each day and do very, very mundane things that seemingly have little to do with a rose, an ear of corn, or a fine bottle of Chardonnay. But they focus on those hundreds of details, little by little, over the full span of the growing season.

Then, one day it is harvest time. And they rejoice in what their persistence and perseverance have brought about. As Proverbs says of this kind of diligence: "Lazy hands make a man poor, but diligent hands bring wealth" (10:4 NIV). And, "the sluggard craves and gets nothing, but the desires of the diligent are fully satisfied" (13:4 NIV).

None of this is rocket science; it is the created order. It is how everything of value comes about, from Honda motorcars to losing a hundred pounds. All goals are achieved through the diligent practice of the day-to-day, mundane tasks.

So, today as you think of your goal, think also of the process required to get you there. If your goal is to lose weight, think of this principle so it will motivate you to go do that forty-five-minute workout. If your goal is a good relationship, think of the value of the process as you make that little sacrifice one more time to work things out. If your goal is a better business, think of this principle as you work out one more problem or make one more cold call. If your goal is to find a relationship, keep it in mind as you go on one more blind date or join one more dating service.

You get the idea. But remember, achieving your goal is a matter of where you put your focus. Keep your eye on the goal, of course. But, also keep your *hands on the plow*, each and every day, and focus today on what you have to do to get there. Do the same thing tomorrow, and the next day, and the day after that. As the successful members of AA who overcome their addictions say at the end of the meeting: "Keep coming back. It works." That admonition holds true about most things of value.

THE WHOLE PICTURE

One thing to remember about the principle of perseverance is that it does not operate in a vacuum. Persistence must be applied alongside all the other principles we have presented in this book. Blind persistence can be just "doing the same thing over and over expecting different results." It could be diligence in simply banging your head against the wall, and that will produce nothing for you but a headache.

So as you persist, examine your thinking. Get connected to the support you need to make it through the process. Work through the failures and learn from them. Take ownership of the results and see them as your problem. Say no to the things that are in the way. Take new steps and risks. All of these steps work together, and as they do, something else happens:

You find that the result is not the only prize! The real prize is the growth that you have realized on your journey. It is the person you have become, and the people you have touched along the way. It is the maturity you have achieved and the lessons you have learned. As James 1:4 says, "Perseverance must finish its work so that you may be mature and complete, not lacking anything." That is the cool thing about "keeping on." You become a better person.

I have come to believe that God can get most of what he needs to get done on the earth without any particular individual. But he gives us the chance to be involved in whatever task he puts in our hands, not only to get it done, but also to grow us up. We are his "workmanship," he says. We are his children, and he uses whatever work we do or whatever situations we find ourselves in to make us better people. More able to love him and more able to love others. More able to bring about lasting fruit as a result of our character growth. Many times we are where we are, doing the job we are doing or the tasks we are involved in because he is growing some aspect of who we are. And even when bad things happen that are not part of his plan, he promises to be with us as we persevere, to help us grow and heal from whatever this fallen world throws at us. As they say, whatever doesn't kill us only makes us stronger.

So learn something that real winners find to be true: *the journey is more valuable than the prize.* It is the trip getting there that we call "life." And in life, we are meant to grow and become who we are supposed to be. Persist, persevere, and grow. Not only will you get the prize, but you will also learn to enjoy the growth process itself and see it as a wonderful journey—an unexpected prize in its own right as you become a better person. Enjoy the trip!

Conclusion

You have read the eight principles of the No-Excuse Plan. What now?

If the material in this book has made sense to you, then you probably are ready to get out of the "blame game," conquer your fears, and set out to achieve your dreams. In telling you that you can do this, we are not simply giving you a motivational pep talk or encouraging wishful thinking. We see it being done every day by people who take ownership over their lives.

You are probably aware that you will need to do some work, such as getting out of your comfort zone or taking ownership of your problems and difficulties or renouncing a victim mentality that has had you stuck. This sort of work is worth all the effort you give it, and it can bear great fruit for your life.

At the same time, it's reasonable for you to ask, "Is there a guarantee that my efforts will pay off? I'm being asked to do some things that are new and different for me. What can I expect in return?"

Your chances of having the better life you want are exponentially greater as you use the principles in this book. *They really do work.* They are proven principles that have changed the lives of many people over many years. But there can be no 100-percent guarantee. There is always risk involved. We hope, however, that you are now less averse to risk than you might have been before reading this book.

At the same time, there is a negative guarantee that applies to all of us. It is sobering, it is certain, and we can depend on it. The negative guarantee is this: If we continue to blame others for our present situation, and if we continue to be afraid to take ownership of our lives, we will also continue to experience the same failures and frustrations that we have always experienced. To the extent that you avoid responsibility for yourself, you will also find your life goals eluding you.

Blame, and the *It's-not-my-fault* mentality, can be somewhat comforting. They work like an anesthetic, temporarily numbing us to the burden of ownership of our lives. But all anesthetics wear off in time, and the comfort of blame always dissipates in the light of what we truly desire. It's much better to embrace the pain of ownership and reap a great life than to be diverted by blame's tempting message.

The Spiritual Design

The idea of a better life isn't something people just conjure up in their heads. Conceiving of a better life is inherent in our design and makeup. God designed you for meaning, purpose, and fulfillment. He put inside you the potential to enter life and, with his guidance, to make something of it. There is a plan for you. While this plan is lodged deep within you, it also originated outside of you in the very mind of God: "'For I know the plans I have for you,' says the Lord. 'They are plans for good and not for disaster, to give you a future and a hope.'"[1] Our welfare, a positive future, a reason for hope, and freedom from calamity are all part of the better life God wants for us, and he has structured things so that you can enter this life. He plays his part in orchestrating events, supporting, and guiding you. You are to play yours in choosing and following the right way, the way of ownership and responsibility for your choices and path.

DREAM ON

So how do you begin? Always start with your dreams and desires. That is where you have the most leverage and payoff. What do you dream about? What do you hope for? What do you want to happen?

For most of us, the answers to these questions come in two parts: We want to receive the good, and we want to remove the bad. We have positive desires and goals for life accomplishments and relationship success. At the same time, we want to avoid, resolve, and end those negative things that bind us, keep us unhappy, and consume valuable time and energy. As in sports, we have to play offense—achieving the dreams and desires, but we also need a defense—overcoming the obstacles and removing the bad stuff that hampers us.

You may have stopped dreaming, setting goals, and planning a long time ago. You may have become discouraged. Or you may have become resigned to thinking that things will never change. No one came blame you for becoming discouraged; that happens to all of us. But discouragement is simply a sign that the path you have taken isn't working for you. There is very likely another path that will work better. Allow yourself to dream and hope again, this time with an openness to the knowledge that good things can happen.

Asking and Answering Yourself

When we begin to dream, hope, and set goals, certain specifics of our lives that we care about start coming to mind. You will often find several areas of your life in which blame, passivity, and fear have taken hold. It can be helpful to look at each of these areas and ask yourself, *How am I contributing to my unhappiness here?* It's one of the most empowering questions you can ever ask.

We have chosen five critical areas of life in which blame or *it's not my fault* thinking can be particularly destructive. In each of these areas, we provide examples of the blame-game thinking that may underlie the problem. After the example, we show a way to approach the problem from an ownership standpoint. We hope these examples will spur your thinking and lead you to take positive action in these areas.

CRITICAL AREA NO. 1: LOVE

Love is one of the greatest and most important experiences that anyone can have. It is a gift, and it can fill up our lives. We all possess a deep desire to have someone connected to our hearts in a safe and growing relationship.

You may be single and looking for the right person, or you may be married and wanting your connection to be happier, deeper, and more intimate. In either situation, a healthy, safe, exciting, and positive love relationship is an important part of life. Or at a more serious level, things may not be going well in your love life. Your dating life may be in trouble, or it may be nonexistent. Your marriage may be empty or struggling with a great deal of pain and conflict.

Avoid the blame game and ask, *What part have I played in this situation?* Here are some common answers to this question and some solutions based on the eight principles we've presented in this book:

- I have blamed my unhappiness on my spouse's (or, boyfriend or girlfriend's) lack of change. *I can become happy even if he (or she) never changes.*

- I have given up too soon. *I can stick to a good plan even if the going gets rough.*

- I have not been clear about what I want and need. *I can let her (or him) know, kindly but directly, what I want and need.*

- I have been afraid to confront. *I can learn how to confront in love and truth.*

- I have avoided looking at my own lack of love or my control issues in the relationship. *I can take responsibility for not being loving or for being controlling, and I can change those things*

- I have put up with things I should never have tolerated. *I can say no to bad treatment and take steps to set limits on how I am treated.*

- I have allowed myself to be alone in this problem. *I can reach out and connect with people who will be my support system.*

In your own life you may find attitudes and answers other than the ones we've listed here. The point is, when you are the one taking action and changing, you have movement toward your goal—a thing that can't happen when you are stuck in blame. Remember, no one else but you can do this for yourself.

Critical Area No. 2: Work

We all want to have a meaningful and fulfilling work life. We want a vocation that both challenges us and fits our area of competence. But problems often arise. Perhaps you find yourself on the wrong career path. Or maybe you're on the right path, but you're not as far along on it as you want to be at this point in life. Maybe you are in the right industry or company, but you haven't advanced as you intended. Or perhaps you see yourself in a different industry. Or you may be questioning everything about your work, wondering where in the world you do fit in.

It's-not-my-fault thinking can keep people paralyzed in their work for decades. The boss, the supervisor, the economy all get blamed, but the one really suffering is you. No one would deny that bosses and economic ups and downs are very important factors, but there are always things you can change in your own life. Let's look again at several blame-game answers that don't work and show the "take control" alternative that can make a difference:

- I have waited for the boss to recognize my merits. *I can set up a meeting with him to make sure he knows what I am doing.*

- I have not taken ownership of any attitudes I have brought to the workplace that have made me difficult to work with. *I can ask for feedback and change what I need to change.*

- I have not sought out more training and experience to develop my marketability. *I can find time and ways to do that and still work for a living.*

- I have not approached my supervisor and tried to work out misunderstandings. *I can take the initiative and let her know that I want to be a team player and help her achieve her goals.*

- I have blamed my company instead of looking at what I can do to help it grow and prosper. *I can choose to be part of the solution, not part of the problem.*

- I have been afraid to be creative. *I can brainstorm and stop playing it safe.*

- I have started new ideas and not followed up on them. *I can stick to it even if the initial response isn't very positive.*

- I have been afraid to try out new jobs and opportunities. *I can look around and see what else is out in the workplace that might fit my abilities and dreams.*

The job market responds not only to talent, but also to ownership and initiative. I have seen many people who weren't the most innately gifted achieve higher success than their more talented colleagues, because they looked at themselves and made the right changes.

Critical Area No. 3: Parenting

If you have children, you know how much you want to see them succeed, make and keep good friends, and become responsible people. To see a child launch into adulthood and do well is the greatest hope of every parent. At the same time, all sorts of obstacles stand in the way of good parenting. A preschooler becomes aggressive with his sibling. A schoolgirl doesn't make the grades she is capable of. A teen struggles with drugs or alcohol.

The problem is often compounded by the reality that the person with the problem isn't really concerned about it. You care more about the issue than your kid does. You're alone in this. Your child isn't coming to you and saying, "Help me." This can lead to a sense of helplessness and discouragement.

Remember that even if your child doesn't know it, he needs you, and he needs you to help him with this problem. Be a parent who takes initiative, and explore these areas in which you may have failed . . . and consider the ownership alternative:

- I have blamed my child and avoided seeing my part in creating the problem he's facing. *I can change the way I parent him so that he has a better chance to succeed.*

- I have been afraid of her anger or of hurting her feelings. *I can learn not to take her negative reactions personally.*

- I have given up too easily when he has resisted me. *I can persist in my rules and discipline, knowing that success will take time.*

- I have not wanted to look at the failures, because they might indicate

I'm not a good parent. *I can deal with my failures without guilt or shame—they provide a way for me to learn how to improve.*

- I have not reached out to others for help. *I can be humble and ask good people for support and advice.*

- I have given in to the mentality that that's just the way she is. *I can give her the gift of knowing she can be a better person, just like I can.*

The best parents aren't those who have all the answers. They are those who take ownership of the problem and go find the answers. When you own your part in the problem, you are then able to help your child own his part as well. He also learns the value of responsibility and ownership.

Critical Area No. 4: Relationships

The person with great relationships is the wealthiest person in the world. Friendships and family connections are a central part of a truly meaningful and purposeful life; their value can't be overestimated. You are highly blessed when you have safe, solid folks who are there for you.

Most people have struggles, minor or major, in their personal relationships. You and a friend have a disagreement that escalates. A relationship ends. You discover that you're picking the wrong people for your friends. Or you find control dynamics in your family that leave you feeling powerless and unhappy.

Look at a few of the typical causes of relationship problems below and consider the suggestions for taking ownership:

- I have silently blamed people without speaking up. *I can tell them what is wrong so they have a chance to hear me and change.*

- I have assumed that people will never change, so I have given up. *I can give them the same grace I'd like them to give me.*

- I need their approval so badly that I could not imagine saying anything that might drive them away. *I can get my approval needs met from other people so that I can be stronger and less emotionally dependent.*

- I have judged them. *I can give up judgment to God and ask for mercy for them and for myself.*

- I have held them to a standard that is not reasonable. *I can be realistic with my expectations of them.*

- I have avoided looking at how I affect them. *I can ask them how I affect them and change what needs to be changed.*

You will find freedom in these explorations. Taking ownership of the relational problem may go a long way toward healing your difficult connection with a friend or family member.

CRITICAL AREA NO. 5: BAD HABITS AND PERSONAL ISSUES

Your dream may be to become a free person—to be free of a habit, addiction, or life pattern that drains you and keeps you in prison. There are many of these potential prisons, ranging from the merely troubling to the life-threatening. Depression, eating problems, anger issues, anxiety, drugs and alcohol struggles, and sexual dependencies are but a few examples. These can discourage and paralyze a person's potential to have the better life he or she was designed to experience.

If you find yourself dealing with these or similar issues, look at the following ways in which you may have passed the blame, and consider what you might do to take control:

- I have waited for others to see how they have caused this problem in me. *I can choose to heal whether or not they ever recognize their negative effect on me.*

- I have blamed God for not protecting me. *I can let go of blame, knowing he has suffered with me and identifies with my pain.*[2]

- I have used the habit or issue as a way to medicate pain, so I have resisted giving it up. *I can face the hurt and pain underneath so that I can be free.*

- When others have tried to connect with me, I have dismissed their efforts. *I can take the risk to let good people inside to love and support me.*

- I have seen myself as different so that no one can truly understand my situation. *I can realize that there are people who "get it" about me, and they can help.*

- Rather than seeing myself as one who has been victimized in my past, I have taken on a victim identity and remained passive. *I can renounce the victim identity and take on my own identity as a person who has both baggage and blessings.*

No one who understands these struggles would ever blame the

person caught in their grip for having personal difficulties. Anger and anxiety issues, eating problems, and addictions almost always involve some combination of being hurt and avoiding the pain necessary to heal. You need others to show compassion for your hurt, to love you, and to encourage you to take ownership of the healing. This is the path of growth that results in deep and permanent change and transformation.

Don't Go It Alone

A word of encouragement: if you want to see better and more significant changes in taking ownership, you must get connected. Find a few people, or even one, to read this book with, or even just to discuss the ideas in it. Relationship is a powerful change agent. It multiplies the effects of any thought or effort you put into these principles. The support, safety, feedback, and help you get from the right people will make a great deal of difference.

And finally, remember that God is for you in making these changes. He is on your side, and he is walking with you, guiding you, and taking you down the path that he designed for you: "The LORD says, 'I will guide you along the best pathway for your life. I will advise you and watch over you' ."[3] Ask him for his help and put your trust in his ways.

God bless you!

Dr. Henry Cloud
Dr. John Townsend
Los Angeles, 2006

Endnotes

Chapter 1: You Can Own Your Own Life
1. To view the district judge's opinion in this case, go online to fl1.findlaw.com/news.findlaw.com/cnn/docs/mcdonalds/plmnmcd12203opn.pdf.

Chapter 2: You Can Learn to Think Differently
1. For more principles and tips to help in this area, see our book, *Rescue Your Love Life: Changing Those Dumb Attitudes & Behaviors That Will Sink Your Marriage* (Nashville, TN: Integrity Publishers, 2005).

Chapter 3: You Can Always Find a Choice
1. For a full treatment of this topic, see *How To Get A Date Worth Keeping*, by Henry Cloud (Grand Rapids, MI: Zondervan, 2005).
2. I suggested my book *Changes That Heal* (Grand Rapids, MI: Zondervan, 1992 rev. ed.).

Chapter 4: You Can Stretch and Risk
1. See Matthew 16:18.
2. For help in this area see our book, *How to Have that Difficult Conversation You've Been Avoiding* (Grand Rapids, MI: Zondervan, 2006).

Chapter 5: You Can Get Connected
1. See Matthew 16:21–23 NIV
2. See Matthew 16:25 NIV
3. See John 3:3–7 NIV
4. See Luke 17:21 NIV
5. See John 2:18–22 NIV
6. See Matthew 5:4 NIV

Chapter 6: You Can Learn to Say No
1. See www.teamhoyt.com.
2. Galatians 6:5 NIV; for more in-depth information about resolving codependency in relationships, see our book, *Boundaries: When to Say Yes, When to Say No to Take Control of Your Life* (Grand Rapids, MI:: Zondervan, 2004).

Chapter 7: You Can Deal with Failure

1. See Romans 8:28.
2. To find a site near you, go online at http://www.cloudtownsend.com/4mns.htm or call (800) 676-4673.

Chapter 8: You Can Persist and Persevere

1. See http://www.bspage.com/1article/peo23.html www.bspage.com/1article/peo23.html.
2. See Proverbs 13:12.

Conclusion

1. Jeremiah 29:11 (NLT)
2. See Hebrews 4:15
3. Psalm 32:8 (NLT)

EMBARK ON A
LIFE-CHANGING JOURNEY
OF PERSONAL AND SPIRITUAL GROWTH

DR. HENRY CLOUD   **DR. JOHN TOWNSEND**

Dr. Henry Cloud and Dr. John Townsend have been bringing hope and healing to millions for over two decades. They have helped people everywhere discover solutions to life's most difficult personal and relational challenges. Their material provides solid, practical answers and offers guidance in areas such as *personal growth, relationships, parenting, dating, marriage* and *career.* Their organization, Cloud-Townsend Resources, can be reached online at www.cloudtownsend.com or by calling 800-676-HOPE (4673).

In addition to their writing, the doctors conduct a unique weekly event called **Solutions** in Southern California. They deliver a powerful message of hope, truth and growth in relationships and life. These compassionate, informative and entertaining presentations are then broadcast via satellite to churches all over the USA and in other countries through Church Communication Network (CCN). These talks can be used for community outreach, small groups or relational ministries. Contact us for information on how your church can subscribe to this series.

The Solutions talks also comprise an extensive audio and video library. For a complete list of all their books, videos, audio tapes and small group resources, contact us.

Drs. Cloud and Townsend have been conducting popular and life-changing seminars for many years on a wide variety of relational and personal topics, from their best-selling *Boundaries* series to relationships, growth, self-help and leadership. Please contact us for information on becoming a host or seminar partner for an event.

Also, if you are a leader and want to grow in your vision and skills, Drs. Cloud and Townsend have developed and operate *Ultimate Leadership,* a week-long intensive leadership workshop in Southern California. Several times a year, the workshop is held for leaders in business, ministry and all walks of life for a time of growth, development and improvement. Contact us for more information.

www.cloudtownsend.com • Call (800) 676-HOPE (4673)

CPSIA information can be obtained at www.ICGtesting.com
Printed in the USA
LVOW08s1312130515

438303LV00003B/7/P